The Book Of Chakras

The Complete Guide To Awaken, Open AndBalance The Chakras For Complete Self- Healing With Meditation And Stones

2 Books in 1:

Chakra Opening

Chakra Stones

Jay K. Morley

© Copyright 2020 by Jay. K. Morley. All right reserved.

No part of this book can be transferred or replicated in any form, which includes print, electronic, photocopying, scanning, mechanical, or recording without subsequent written permission from the author.

While the author has taken the utmost efforts to ensure the accuracy of the written content, all readers are advised to follow the information stated therein at their own risk. The author will not be held responsible for any individual or economic damage caused by the misunderstanding of information. All readers of this book are encouraged to seek expert advice when required.

This book has been written for informational purposes only. Efforts have been made to make this book as comprehensive and precise as possible. Nevertheless, there may be mistakes in typography or content. Also, this book provides information only up to the publishing date. Therefore, this book should be used as a guide - not as the ultimate source.

The primary purpose of this book is to teach readers about the topic being discussed. The writer and the publisher do not warrant that the information contained in this book is comprehensive and will not be held responsible for any errors or oversights. The writer and publisher will have neither accountability nor blame to any individual or object in regards to any loss or damage which is caused or alleged to be caused directly or indirectly through this book.

Table of Contents

PART ONE

Introduction 11
Chapter 1: The Significance of Chakras in Your Life 13
    The Importance of Chakras in Human Life 15
    How are Chakras Linked to the Human Body? 17
Chapter 2: The Seven Chakras and their Functions 19
    What are the Seven Chakras? 19
    Functions of the Crown Chakra 20
    Functions of the Third Eye Chakra 21
    Functions of the Throat Chakra 22
    Functions of the Heart Chakra 23
    Functions of the Solar Plexus Chakra 24
    Functions of the Sacral Chakra 25
    Functions of the Root Chakra 26
    How to Awaken the Chakras? 27
Chapter 3: Why are the Chakras Blocked? 30
    What Exactly is a Chakra Blockage? 31
    What are the Main Causes of Chakra Blockages? 33
Chapter 4: Heal Your Chakras 36
    Benefits of Chakra Healing 37
        Improves Physical Health and Well-Being 37
        Enhances Spiritual Fitness 37
        Removes Bad Energy Stored in the Body 38
        Imparts Love and Joy in One's Life 38
        Allows You to Become Aware of Your Inner Self 39
        Transforms Your Weakness into Your Strength 40
        Gives Access to Financial Wisdom 40
        Inspires You to Turn Dreams into Reality 41
        Gives You Intuition 41
        Helps in Expressing and Releasing Emotions in a Healthy Manner 42
Chapter 5: Heal Your Chakras Using Crystals 44
    How Can Crystals Help Us Heal Chakras? 44
    What Are Some Useful Crystals? 46

The Root Chakra Crystals..46
The Sacral Chakra Crystals 46
The Solar Plexus Chakra Crystals...47
The Heart Chakra Crystals 47
The Throat Chakra Crystals 48
The Third Eye Chakra Crystals 48
The Crown Chakra Crystals..49

Chapter 6: How to Know If Your Chakras are Out of Balance? 50
    The Main Symptoms and Signs of Blocked Chakras and the Problems Caused By It...50
        Blocked Root Chakra...52
        Blocked Sacral Chakra...52
        Blocked Solar Plexus Chakra...53
        Blocked Heart Chakra 53
        Blocked Throat Chakra..53
        Blocked Third Eye Chakra 54
        Blocked Crown Chakra 54
    Main Symptoms and Signs of Overactive Chakras and the Problems Caused By It...54
        An Overactive Root Chakra...55
        An Overactive Sacral Chakra...55
        An Overactive Solar Plexus Chakra.....................................55
        An Overactive Heart Chakra 55
        An Overactive Throat Chakra..56
        An Overactive Third Eye Chakra..56
        An Overactive Crown Chakra 56

Chapter 7: Chakra Balancing...58
    Meditation..58
Affirmations...60
The Root Chakra 60
The Sacral Chakra...60
The Solar Plexus 60
The Heart Chakra 61
The Throat Chakra..61
The Third Eye Chakra 61
The Crown Chakra 61
Colours..61
Sound...62

Essential Oils 62
Chakra Crystals 63
Yoga 64
Once Balanced, How To Keep Chakras From Getting Blocked Or Overactive Again? 66
Role of Healthy Diet and Nutrition to Keep Your Chakras Aligned 69
    Food for the Root Chakra 70
    Food for the Sacral Chakra 70
    Food for the Solar Plexus Chakra 70
Food for the Heart Chakra 71
Food for the Throat Chakra 71
Food for the Third Eye Chakra 71
    Food for the Crown Chakra 72

Chapter 9: Mindfulness 73
The Role of Mindfulness to Keep Your Chakras Balanced 74
Meditation as A Way to Practice Mindfulness 78

Chapter 10: Yoga Poses to Align Your Chakras 80
Seven Yoga Poses to Balance Your Chakras 80
Mountain Pose for Root Chakra 81
    How to Practise 82
Revolved Triangle Pose for Sacral Chakra 82
    How to Practise 83
Boat Pose for Solar Plexus Chakra 84
    How to Practise 85
Low Lunge for Heart Chakra 86
    How to Practise 86
Easy Pose for Throat Chakra 87
    How to Practise 88
Dolphin Pose for the Third Eye Chakra 89
    How to Practise 89
Balancing Butterfly for Crown Chakra 90
    How to Practise 91

Conclusion 93

PART TWO

Introduction 95

- A Brief History of the Chakras 97
- Chakra Basics 99
- **Understanding the Seven Chakras** 102
  - 1st Chakra: Muladhara: "Root Center" 102
  - 2nd Chakra: Svadhishthana: "Abode Of the Self" or "Identity Chakra" 103
  - 3rd Chakra: Manipura: "Gem Center" 104
  - 4th Chakra: Anahata: "Un-Struck" or "Unhurt", Heart Center 105
  - 5th Chakra: Vishuddha: "Control Center" or "Purification" 106
  - 6th Chakra: Ajna: "Third Eye" or "Command Center" 107
  - 7th Chakra: Sahasrara: "Unbound" or "Infinite", the Seat Of The Soul 108
- **Recognizing Imbalances in the Chakras** 111
  - 1st: Muladhara (Root Chakra) 112
  - 2nd: Svadhishthana (Pelvic Chakra) 113
  - 3rd: Manipura (Navel Chakra) 114
  - 4th: Anahata (Heart Chakra) 115
  - 5th: Vishuddha (Throat Chakra) 116
  - 6th: Ajna (Third Eye Chakra) 117
  - 7th: Sahasrara (Crown Chakra) 118
- **Introducing Crystals and Healing Stones** 127
  - Crystals, Minerals, Gemstones 127
  - The Origin of Crystals 127
  - Types of Crystals 128
  - How Do Crystals Work 128
- **A Brief History of Crystals and Healing** 130
  - Amulets 130
  - Historical References 131
  - Crystals in Religion 132
  - The Renaissance 133
    - The Beginning of Crystal Healing 134
    - Crystal and Gemstone Meaning 135
    - A New Age Dawns 136

Different Crystal Shapes ... 137
- Tumbled Stones ... 138
- Spheres ... 138
- Pyramids ... 139
- Harmonizers ... 140
- Cubes ... 140
- Hearts ... 141
- Points ... 141
- Clusters ... 142

The Formation of Crystals ... 143
- What Are Crystals ... 143
- How Are They Formed ... 144
- Crystal Structure ... 146
- What Unique Properties Do Crystals Have? ... 148

Crystal Collection ... 149
- 1. Amethyst ... 149
- 2. Desert Rose Selenite ... 150
- 3. Rose Quartz ... 151
- 4. Hematite ... 151
- 5. Iron Pyrite ... 152
- 6. Tiger Eye ... 152
- 7. Raw Emerald ... 153
- 8. Citrine 153
- 9. Celestine 154
- 10. Clear Quartz ... 154

How to Select Your Crystal and Care for It ... 155
- Select the Best Crystal ... 155
- Ask the Universe to Help You ... 155
- Use Your Intuition ... 156
- Choose the Crystal According to Your Birth Month ... 157
- Experiment with Different Crystals ... 157

Care for Your Crystal ... 157
Water ... 158
Salt Water ... 158

Natural Light 159
Sage 159
Use Other Stones 160
Why Do Chakras Need Healing 161
Chakras and Your Energetic Frequency 162
Balance Is Key in Chakra Healing 164
How Can You Balance Chakras with Crystals? 168
Red Root Chakra 169
Orange Pelvic Charka 169
Yellow Solar Plexus Chakra 169
Green Heart Chakra 169
Blue Throat Chakra 169
Indigo Third Eye Chakra 170
Violet Crown Chakra 170
Place Chakra Crystals on Your Body According to Their Respective Chakras 170
Keep Chakra Crystals Near You While Resting 172
Meditate with Chakra Crystals 172
Wear Crystals 173
Chakra Crystal Healing Tips 174
Functions of Crown Chakra 174
Imbalance in Crown Chakra 174
Healing Crystals 175
Functions of Third Eye Chakra 175
Imbalance in Third Eye Chakra 176
Healing Crystals 176
Functions of Throat Chakra 177
Imbalance in Throat Chakra 177
Healing Crystal 177
Functions of Heart Chakra 178
Imbalance in Heart Chakra 178
Healing Crystal 179
Functions of Solar Plexus Chakra 179
Imbalance in Solar Plexus Chakra 180

    Healing Crystal 180
    Functions of Sacral Chakra 181
    Imbalance in Sacral Chakra 181
    Healing Crystal 182
    Functions of Root Chakra 182
    Imbalance in Root Chakra 183
    Healing Crystals 183
Conclusion 186

Thanks for choosing The Book of Chakras. Be sure to leave a short review on the plat- form where you purchased this book, if you enjoy it. It´s important for me to know what you think about it.

PART ONE

Introduction

Healing and balancing your chakras is an essential part of optimizing your mental and physical health. Being in tune with your energies will allow you to live a wholly peaceful and serene life. Activating and maintaining your chakras' health is next to impossible without knowing the right facts about these wheels of energy.

The seven primary chakras control the bodily regions corresponding to their locations and allow one to feel absolutely at peace when activated. Unfortunately, inevitable stressors in life, such as traumatic incidents and an overload of negative emotions, cause your chakra system to misbalance. Unbalanced chakras can cause you a great deal of mental and physical discomfort. You may fall victim to poor mental health, anxiety, and insecurities. The physical symptoms of a chakra misbalance include issues like chronic pain and your blood pressure heightening.

To realign and heal your chakras, you must take time out of your day to focus on yourself. Make specific changes within your lifestyle. The first step to rebalance your chakras is to understand that something is amiss. This book tells you the signs of chakra blockages and how to remove them. It helps you undertake an arduous journey to heal your chakras with the help of crystals, food, and meditation.

Chapter 1: The Significance of Chakras in Your Life

What are Chakras?

It is said that a change in perspective is the only thing you need to change your life. That's not all true, however. It takes an awful lot of willpower and self-awareness to make a permanent change for the good of your life. You have to know which parts of your life you need to discover, change, and finally rebirth. To bring about an everlasting mental and physical transformation, you need to know about your body's primary energy points. That's where the chakra system comes in.

Originating in the Hindu Vedas' sacred texts in the early 1500s, the chakra system combines elements of psychic energy with your physical well-being. This New Age philosophy has recently gained popularity within the Western world because of its extraordinary health benefits. Not only does the chakra system cater to an individual's physical health, but it also tends to improve a person's emotional welfare.

What exactly is a chakra? There are seven main energy points known as 'chakras' in our bodies that can be activated to strengthen our mental and physical health. The word 'chakra' comes from the Sanskrit word *chakra*, which refers to a "wheel." These chakras are thought of as spinning wheels in different locations of your body, the main ones being the seven that run along your spine. In order to maximize your well-being and mental health, these bundles of energy need to stay open. When activated, they correspond with significant organs, nerves, and areas of our body connected to our physical and emotional health.

There are said to be around 114 total chakras within our bodies, but the main seven lie from our spine's base to the crown of our heads. It is said that our physical, mental, and emotional health is directly linked to the corresponding chakra state. While all the chakras have their distinctive properties, they ultimately work as a system. If one of your chakras is blocked, it affects the performance of the rest of them.

The seven main chakras are as follows:

1) Crown Chakra
2) Third Eye Chakra
3) Throat Chakra
4) Heart Chakra
5) Solar Plexus Chakra
6) Sacral Chakra
7) Root Chakra

Years of accumulated mental stress and unresolved negative emotions tend to misbalance your chakras. Emotions are stored in our bodies, and the negative ones do more harm than good. We live and breathe with uneasiness and discomfort because of these imbalances in our body, without quite knowing why. Throughout our lives, our emotions' negative impacts and consequences slowly amass and come out in harmful ways. They flow through our bodies, resulting in an overload of destructive energy that affects our health in several ways.

It takes a long time to become aware of our destructive traits and work on them, but the chakra system can help erase the discomfort of living with bad health and emotional states.

It's entirely okay to have unbalanced or blocked chakras! Physical and spiritual exercises like yoga and meditation, will help you activate these rolled-up bundles of energy within your body. Activities like these assist in aligning the chakras within your frame, creating a free-flowing channel for your vital life force to flourish through.

The Importance of Chakras in Human Life

Chakras are centers of energy dispersed throughout our bodies, and being in touch with our body is one of the first steps of becoming physically and mentally fit. While this body is just a cage of flesh and bone for some, others understand the importance of taking care of their physical forms. These energy points were named chakras because they represent growth and movement. These complex circles symbolize the dynamics of our shifting energies.

Energy is said to be continually changing, evolving. Our state of mind and our physical health is dependent on our chakras and their states. When balanced, the chakras in our body are situated in such a way that they allow our revitalizing life force to follow a path from the base of our spine to the top of our head. This journey is known to transcend dimensions. There are various yogic activities and spiritual healing practices that allow energy movement to carry on seamlessly and without barriers.

Chakras are some of the most intimate forms of energy in the world. Not only are they within your body, but they are also deeply connected to every state of your being. Spun the right way, the same chakras that result in you craving food and other external items can become completely free of those desires. Transforming these chakras to an evolved state will result in your human body reaching a serenity and peace level that you have never known before.

We are all beings of energy and consciousness, trapped in a corporal form. Our thoughts and feelings are all streams of energy, making their way from our bodies to our minds. As complex as we are with our actions, our emotions and states of mind are simply energy that needs constant revitalization. That is what aligning your chakras does.

How are Chakras Linked to the Human Body?

Although chakras are an ancient concept, their connection with our bodily functions is undeniable even in today's time. Our anatomy has shown a strong association with the seven wheels of energy. Unbalanced chakras manifest themselves in our physical health through heart and weight problems, anxiety, and other insecurities. Blocks in our chakras are sometimes also visible via our actions.

The first of all, chakras within our body, the Root Chakra, is located at our spine's base. This energy wheel is directly associated with the pelvic plexus and the first three vertebrae, which are our physical bodies' very foundation. When blocked, the root chakra manifests itself in physical issues like arthritis and bladder problems. You will also feel emotionally insecure and in need of essential support. Setting this chakra alight means being in touch with your physicality. If only the Root Chakra is activated, things like food and sleep will be your priority. This chakra is incredibly important to keep yourself grounded.

As you can see, your chakras' state is directly related to the state of your health. Your mental and emotional states also depend on your chakras. To achieve optimum health and make the best of your life on Earth, staying in touch with your chakras is essential. Like a plant needs water to survive, your chakras need your attention and patience to spin. It will help if you put in the work.

Going back to the Root Chakra, activities related to the Earth, like gardening, hiking, and consuming healthy food, will help activate this energy point. Practicing these will not just help invigorate your mind, but it will also improve your health by strengthening your core and aiding digestion.

Balancing your chakras means keeping your body and emotions in check. Our emotions are continually flowing through bodies. Certain events trigger an overload of negative emotions, such as heartbreak and trauma. Sometimes it takes years to recover from these events.

Letting your chakras align will allow your mind and body to heal. To become the best version of ourselves, we must learn to bridge the gap between our minds and bodies. We need to undertake a spiritual journey that lets us keep only the most raw and honest emotions. Once your chakras are balanced, your physical health will be better than ever.

Chapter 2: The Seven Chakras and their Functions

What are the Seven Chakras?

You must have heard the phrase "chakras aligning," referring to things like a person lucking out and hitting the jackpot. The truth is that all you need to *hit the jackpot* and make the most of any situation is to be in touch with your chakras. We were born with the power to do great things. We have to unlock that power. To do so, we must align our mental and physical states by balancing our chakras. A healthy chakra system will do wonders for your life.

Have you seen people who seem to have everything figured out? Not only are they in great shape, but they also seem to always be at peace with everything? It is truly an art to learn how to accept changes as they come. Aligning your chakras is like taking a long spiritual journey that allows you to become the very best version of yourself if you succeed in completing. It enables you to let go of your worries and anxieties and improves your physical health in ways you never thought possible. But what steps does that journey entail?

The seven main chakras are the stops you have to make on this journey. These consist of the Crown Chakra, the Third Eye Chakra, the Throat Chakra, the Heart Chakra, the Solar Plexus Chakra, the Sacral Chakra, and the Root Chakra.

Functions of the Crown Chakra

The Crown Chakra, or the highest chakra, sits just atop your head at the crown. It is a problematic chakra to activate– only a small amount of people are ever able to. Known as the *Sahastrar* in Sanskrit, this chakra is represented by the color violet, which is said to be the color of one's connection with divine energies. This vortex of energy is said to define an individual's spiritual association with God or the Creator of the universe. The Crown Chakra is incomplete without balancing the other chakras, and is known to control one's inner and outer beauty. The *Sahastrar* matures with us as we grow. Once fully developed, this chakra allows us to rid ourselves of the conventional boundaries we have caged ourselves within and consider our existence an integral part of this universe.

Also called the Chakra of Enlightenment, the Crown Chakra is linked mainly to our brain and nervous system. Once this chakra is opened, one's life embodies serenity and peace. We achieve a level of calm previously unknown to us and start living in the present. The spinning of this wheel of energy allows the other chakras to activate more rapidly.

Functions of the Third Eye Chakra

The *Ajna* or the 'Brow' is the Third Eye Chakra located on the forehead, between both the eyes. You will note that the third eye is a symbol of glorious wisdom and insight in modern media and books. The cycle of energy between our eyes is the origin of that. The Third Eye Chakra allows us to see beyond a surface-level view. It is connected to intuition, imagination, and an astute perception of the world and life itself.

A blockage in this chakra manifests itself as headaches and concentration problems. Your vision and hearing may also be affected if your *Ajna* is in poor health. Opening this energy center allows you to have increased foresight and vision.

The 'Eye of the Soul' the Third Eye Chakra, once balanced, will provide you with a heightened sense of self. You will be able to perceive things beyond the obvious and transcend to another level of reality.

Functions of the Throat Chakra

The third stop on our spiritual journey is the Throat Chakra or the *Vishuddha* (meaning 'pure'). Situated on the throat level, near the spine, this energy vortex is associated with the thyroid, esophagus, and upper vertebrae in the physical body. The *Vishudda* controls one's expression of self, communication, and connection with oneself and others.

Our throats are what pave the way for our voices to be heard. We make our path in this world through the power of speech. Once born into this realm, we cry to show our discomfort. Our ability to speak shows our growth and perfects as we mature. Our maturity is defined by our expression of the thoughts we create within our minds. The Throat Chakra is connected to all of these.

An unbalanced Throat Chakra affects our thyroid and, in turn, our mood. We experience unstable emotions and mood swings that leave us bothered and disturbed. Activating this Chakra is hard work, but once achieved, it will allow us to assert and project ourselves with a balance of good communication and a healthy mental state.

Functions of the Heart Chakra

An essential step down the chakra system, the Heart Chakra is positioned at the center of our chest, right above our hearts. This chakra is deeply associated with the concept of self-love and an individual's ability to give and receive love. Its Sanskrit name, *Anahata,* means 'unhurt' or 'boundless.'

People with a blocked Heart Chakra will find it hard to open up to others and experience love. Another result of a blockage in this chakra is an individual's inability to let go of the hurt. People with an unbalanced *Anahata* will hold on to resentment and experience feelings of loneliness and disconnection from others. They may also go through heart and lung problems, along with weight issues. This energy bundle is crucial to overcome on the journey to activate all chakras as it bridges the gap between the higher and lower ones.

The Heart Chakra can be activated by practicing yogic healing and repeating positive affirmations of love to oneself. Once fully balanced, the *Anahata* will allow one to immerse themselves in deep compassion and empathy fully. It will enable a healthy stream of love and inner serenity to flow through your body, unfiltered.

Functions of the Solar Plexus Chakra

The Solar Plexus Chakra is connected to our confidence and self-control. Located in the abdominal area between one's navel and solar plexus, this energy center is associated with the digestive system, the pancreas, and the liver. When in alignment, this chakra allows one to be free to express their true self.

An unbalancing of this chakra results in feeling a devastating amount of shame and insecurity. You use this chakra when you gather the courage to do something daring and feel butterflies in your stomach. This bundle of psychic energy is directly responsible for your self-esteem and self-worth. Blockages in this chakra can also cause ulcers, eating disorders, indigestion, and other digestive issues.

The Solar Plexus Chakra is a connection from the gut to the brain. Overcoming the hurdles present in the path to achieving an open Solar Plexus Chakra will allow you to awaken your real being and express your every intention without doubt.

Functions of the Sacral Chakra

The Sacral Chakra or the *Swadisthana* is linked to our perception of emotions, both ours and other people's. This chakra is positioned at our lower abdomen, two inches below the navel. Because of its location being the pelvic region, this bundle of energy is directly responsible for our pleasure and sexuality. It also controls our sense of fulfillment and well-being.

When this chakra is unaligned, it causes a loss of control within our lives. It causes kidney, bladder, and adrenal gland problems. As our adrenal glands are the source of stress and anxiety, an uneven chakra will not just affect your mental state but also restrict your ability to make rational decisions.

Controlling your water intake and practicing healing yoga can help you regain control of your Sacral Chakra and discover immense creative power and sexual energy. Unlocking this chakra will lead you to a life of intensity and pleasure.

Functions of the Root Chakra

The Root Chakra or the *Muladhara* is located at the base of the spine, in the tailbone region. It controls our survival instincts, such as financial savings and food. When blocked, it results in us feeling unsafe and threatened by all kinds of circumstances. To fully align all your chakras, opening the Root Chakra is essential.

Once it is open, the *Muladhara* allows us to feel confident and stand our ground while facing challenges. The spine base is also connected to our feelings of safety and security because it is the very foundation of our physical form.

Blockages in this chakra can result in arthritis, digestive problems, and experiencing an overload of insecurity and lack of focus. It may also result in codependency, as the individual has a severe lack of self-esteem. Activating this chakra can be hard work, but once opened, it allows us to experience life freely and without any pressing needs or desires.

How to Awaken the Chakras?

It would not be a stretch to say that energy governs our lives. We are simply beings of energy inside a physical form. To awaken the chakras, we need to undertake a full spiritual and physical cleanse. Our chakras are what connect our physical body with our mental and emotional states. They contribute to our well-being in several ways. To align your chakras and let them heal you from within, you have to brace yourself for a few months of effort.

To awaken the Root Chakra, you will have to face your fears and bring them into the light. Acknowledging them is the first step, followed by allowing yourself to uncover all parts of you that you have hidden from others and yourself. Use feelings of compassion and love to release your fears into the universe.

To awaken the Sacral Chakra, one must let go of all feelings of shame and guilt inside of them. You must learn to forgive your past mistakes and love yourself. Understand that your mistakes have made you a wiser and stronger person, and that you are brave for coming to terms with them.

To activate your Solar Plexus Chakra, release all of your disappointments and regrets into this world. Accept all your flaws and the fact that they are a crucial part of who you are.

For your Heart Chakra to open up, you must allow your grief to course through you one final time before you let it out into this world. Respect that your emotions are valid and that the loss and hurt you have experienced will expand your capacity to love in the future.

To awaken the *Vishuddha* or the Throat Chakra, you must let go of all the things you have not allowed yourself to accept. Release all your denials and lies. Allow yourself to see you as you indeed are, in your true nature.

The Third-Eye Chakra is awakened when you break the illusion of separation and become one with all the energy sources surrounding you. It unlocks ultimate freedom.

To awaken your Root Chakra, you must let go of all material attachments. Accepting the fact that letting go of earthly attachments does not mean that they disappear, it´s really important.

Chapter 3: Why are the Chakras Blocked?

Our cultures and lives may be different, but humans follow a single pattern all around the world. Whether you are seated in a plush leather chair in an air-conditioned office room or sitting on a rickety chair in a sweltering hot classroom on the other side of the globe, there isn't much difference in your lifestyles. We may eat different cuisines and live in different regions, we might even wear completely different attires, but our lives are all practically lived the same way: on autopilot.

We routinely get up in the morning, brush our teeth, and go to work. For about thirty years or so, we work to provide for our families to stay at home to care for our children. And then we welcome death. Even without implementing the chakra system, there is no indication that we are aware of ourselves and our surroundings. We don't care about things. We don't stop and stare at oceans or watch the sunrise up at dawn. We go through the motions like automatons.

Being self-aware allows to understand several of your displaced emotions truly. You might feel regret at certain things or an overwhelming repulsion from the thought of a particular activity. Being aware of oneself means taking the time to learn your language and understand your emotions. To live life to the maximum, unlocking the art of self-awareness is essential.

It is where the chakra system comes in.

Awakening your chakras allows you to implement a higher level of self-awareness and balance. It lets you discover your blind spots and heal your past traumas. Once awakened, the chakras within your body will allow you to feel a sense of completeness and freedom. A process known as 'chakra healing' takes place. It uses spiritual healing to improve your physical and emotional health. But to do that, first you have to unlock your blocked chakras.

What Exactly is a Chakra Blockage?

A blocked chakra is when the wheels of energy inside your body are rusty and don't spin well. Maybe you haven't activated them yet, or perhaps you haven't practiced the right yogic activities in a while; either way, blocked chakras can manifest themselves in some very bothersome ways.

Perhaps you have been feeling off lately, or are plagued by specific physical and mental issues like indigestion or anxiety. If these problems carry on for long, that's your cue. Something is messing with your chakras.

A chakra blockage means that the energy flow inside your body is unmoving. You can think of it as a traffic jam. If the cars don't move, it'll take you hours to get to your destination on time. Similarly, the energy inside of you is at a standstill, unable to flow. When this energy is stuck, the wheels of power inside you can't spin either. You will experience a chakra blockage.

A chakra blockage can be mental, emotional, or even spiritual. Some people believe that specific chakra blockages are karmic or energetic, as well. In Sanskrit, the word karma means 'action.' Certain Eastern religions and philosophies dictate that the actions we take throughout our lifetimes remain with us in a state of karmic energy. Right actions result in good karmic energy and positive vibes, whereas wrong actions can lead to a series of bad luck.

Karma isn't just a single action; it is also the consequence of that action. You must know certain people who always seem to be dealt with the worst cards. This bad luck may be a karmic result of a previous immoral action. The essence of karma is that the energy inside you and the energy surrounding you are aware of your actions. Wicked deeds result in your chakras being blocked as a repayment of the karmic debt.

Blocks in your chakra are like toxins running inside your bloodstream. They may be invisible to the human eye, but they are still quite dangerous. They restrict your body and mind's performance in different ways until you are merely a shadow of your best self.

What are the Main Causes of Chakra Blockages?

A variety of things can cause chakra blockages. As human beings, we are prone to feeling a little lost or overwhelmed at times. Our emotions are connected to our health. An overload of negative emotions will certainly deteriorate an individual's health. But that's not what all negative emotions do. They have a way of seeping into our physical form and mind's cracks, misbalancing our chakras, and making us feel physically and emotionally unwell.

Chakras become unbalanced due to negative energy and psychic debris. Think of your emotional state as a plate that clutters over time with the leftover emotions resulting from experiencing life. Some of these emotions add to your stress, some to anger, and so on. Thus, to achieve mental peace and good emotional health, you must clear that plate now and then.

Fear and various kinds of trauma result in your chakras getting blocked. An inability to deal with the emotions and reality that you are facing will also negatively affect your chakra system's health. It will make you feel like you have lost control of your life and that regaining a sense of autonomy is almost impossible.

Applying too much power to a bulb that requires less voltage will undeniably result in the bulb's fuse blowing. It is because it could not handle the massive surge of electrical power applied to it. The same can be said about our mental states. Human beings are in no way fragile, but a surplus of negative emotions can certainly extinguish the fires of the chakras inside us.

Negative emotions and thoughts are like debris in a clear blue ocean. Accumulating negative emotions over time will restrict the free-flowing movement of the energy inside you, resulting in a blocking of the chakras.

We have already established that chakra blockages can be psychological, but what we will learn now is that our poor physical choices can also displace our chakras. The chakra system's health is heavily reliant on our physical state. We end up creating imbalances in the system by overeating or not eating healthy, avoiding exercise, sitting for too long, and exerting ourselves beyond our capabilities. Poor dietary choices and other lifestyle choices like overworking and abusing drugs can also result in our chakras being blocked.

Another cause of a chakra blockage can be a hindrance to our spiritual health. We must accept the pool of energy and power that sits restlessly inside our corporal bodies. Spiritually rigid individuals who refuse to acknowledge the spiritual aspect of life may experience chakra blocks.

Ultimately, there are many reasons why our chakras may be blocked. The process of unblocking these power cycles inside us requires spiritual, physical, and emotional healing. The first step is to correct your sleeping and eating patterns and let go of excess emotions. If you treat your body like a temple, your chakras will certainly align, and you will live a long and peaceful life.

Chapter 4: Heal Your Chakras

So far, we have discussed a lot about imbalance and blockage in chakras and the problems caused due to them. In this part of the book, we will explain everything related to chakras healing. First of all, we must understand that no one in this world has completely balanced chakras except those who have achieved the highest stage in meditation, i.e., Samadhi. The rest of the people battle with their everyday struggles, anxiety, and stress because their chakras are imbalanced or blocked. The good news is we can realign our chakras to function well using different methods such as meditation, affirmations, massage, color association, music, essential oils, and chakra crystals. We will discuss the details of each healing process in the upcoming chapters. We can choose any one or a combination of a few of these methods to heal our chakras.

Chakra healing may be a new concept for you, and you may not be aware of the benefits it can pose in your life. However, investing in chakras healing will be one of the best decisions you will ever make for yourself. Below are some of the benefits of chakras healing that can bring a dramatic transformation in your life.

Benefits of Chakra Healing

Improves Physical Health and Well-Being

Chakras are the primary sources of energy and vital centers which pass on the life force to different parts of the body. Just imagine that your arteries are cluttered and blocked. What will happen then? It will obstruct blood flow. When blood doesn't flow to all the organs properly, it will result in various health issues such as chest pain, shortness of breath, numbness, and cardiac diseases. The same is the case with chakras. When your chakras are blocked or imbalanced, the energy doesn't flow well through your body. Hence it causes different physical and mental health issues. There are several reasons for blockages in chakras, such as negative thoughts, overthinking, fears, overconsuming unhealthy food, lack of physical activity, and poor habits. Chakras directly influence the physical, mental, emotional, and spiritual well-being of an individual. Balancing your chakras can help you improve your physical health and well-being.

Enhances Spiritual Fitness

Just like physical health, spiritual fitness is also essential for our bodies to stay stable and calm. Spiritual and emotional issues have a powerful effect on everything we do in all aspects of our lives. Chakras serve as the boundary between the spiritual realms and the physical body. This boundary needs to be balanced to maintain the balance in the human body. Every chakra holds a spiritual aspect, and as you move from bottom to top while healing your chakras, it pushes you to a step ahead on the spiritual ladder and unfolds the hidden realms of spirituality in front of you.

Removes Bad Energy Stored in the Body

Chakra balancing and healing help you live a healthier lifestyle, not only in terms of physical health but also in emotional and mental health by keeping your body and mind relaxed. When your chakras are balanced, you can play a constructive role in maintaining your relationship. Moreover, balanced chakras allow you to grow financially. Chakras, when aligned, promote the elimination of toxins from the body. It is essential to apply chakra clearing techniques regularly, and you'll feel relaxed and clear.

Imparts Love and Joy in One's Life

Aligning your chakras, especially sacral chakra, imparts love and joy in your life. In the literature, the purpose of the sacral chakra is mentioned as life energy and creativity. It is associated with vitality and fulfillment.

People with a balanced and open sacral chakra are usually active, resilient, and willing to face life challenges. They embrace change without getting affected by them adversely. People with balanced sacral chakra love art and nature and can experience joy and analyze their emotions without being overwhelmed and worried. People with open sacral chakra are usually spontaneous. If you haven't experienced any such feelings in the near past, your chakras might be blocked, and you need to work on them to inculcate love and joy in your life.

Allows You to Become Aware of Your Inner Self

When you become enlightened about your chakras and get them healed, balanced, and aligned, you can feel your conscience and gain control over your thoughts. When our chakras are not balanced, our thoughts and emotions drive our actions. However, when our chakras are healed, we are in the driver's seat and control our emotions. We become aware of our inner selves and realize the purpose of coming to this world to meet the supreme consciousness. This realization helps us get over the worldly desires and greed, anger, jealousy, and all damaging emotions. Chakra healing helps us achieve our real objective of coming into this world.

Transforms Your Weakness into Your Strength

Whenever we come across a negative experience, we cause the associated chakra energy to block that energy. Similarly, suppose we are holding on to negative emotions such as self-blaming, self-pitying due to our inability to deal with or move on in life. In that case, we block the chakras, requiring healing and balancing.

As we open and heal our chakras through self-healing methods or by consulting a professional healer, energy begins to flow freely once again, and things get back to normal in our lives. When the energy moves freely throughout the body, we become able to turn negative in to positive. We don't consider our weaknesses as our failure. Instead, we embrace them and strive to turn them into our strengths.

Gives Access to Financial Wisdom

Many professional healers explain that with constant affirmations, you can turn your life. When healing your chakras on your own, you can do daily affirmations to keep them balanced. When your mind is decluttered from all negative emotions, your intelligence and intellect will grow. Moreover, when you affirm that you are getting money from different sources and create ways to get it as per your plan, you will be able to manifest it. According to Chakra healers, money blocks are beliefs that interrupt the pattern of free-flowing energy. So, to eliminate these money blocks, we need to let the energy pass through our bodies.

Root and Sacral chakras are said to be responsible for our finances. When these chakras are balanced, our bodies allow the energy to pass and unblock all the financial blocks. So, to resolve financial matters and overcome money blocks, you must keep your first two chakras aligned and working.

Inspires You to Turn Dreams into Reality

When our chakras get healed, we establish a strong connection with the real potential in this universe. By clearing our body and energy system through self-healing or with professional healers' help, we come in a better position to bring the mind and the body together in one space. It will smooth our transformation process and will help us accomplish our goals. In fact, through chakra healing, we become mindful of our strengths and weaknesses. Thus, we can benefit from our strengths and work on overcoming our weaknesses.

Gives You Intuition

Intuition is the inner voice that nudges you when something is wrong, or you are about to make an important decision. It is an internal force that lets you discover your divine self.

When your chakras, especially crown and heart chakras, are well-balanced, you can summon your intuition with your own will, instead of waiting for it to come to you. Awakening your intuitive voice helps you:

- Slow down your thought process and keep yourself calm in all situations.
- Think positive and establish your positive energy aura.
- Release everything that ruins your peace of mind.
- Feel positive energy entering your body and negative energy leaving your body.

Helps in Expressing and Releasing Emotions in a Healthy Manner

Chakra healing allows positive energy to flow in the body. Hence, it releases the unwanted negative energy, helping you get rid of distressing emotions and thoughts. This process can lead a person into a state of fulfillment, both physically and emotionally. Cleansing the energy systems and unleashing the trapped energy results in emotional stability in the body. It helps you regain your lost self-confidence and self-control. As a result, you are better positioned to express your emotions, healthily and constructively.

Above mentioned are just a few benefits that you can yield through chakra healing. There are numerous other advantages that you will experience when you start working on your chakras. In the next chapter, I will discuss all the methods and techniques you can adopt to begin self-healing your chakras. Apart from them, many professional chakra healers can help you accomplish your goal.

Chapter 5: Heal Your Chakras Using Crystals

One way to cleanse and revitalize your chakras is to use healing crystals. Crystals possess high frequencies and can lift the vibrations of our chakras to clear them. Put merely; healing crystals help your chakras spin at an optimal rate. They have a positive impact on your mental and physical health in many ways.

Crystals have a brilliant array of energetic properties. The idea of healing with crystals stems from the fact that specific stones have the power to magnify and balance the energy centers within your body. It has a profound effect on our well-being.

Each crystal has its unique attribute and can be used strategically to activate blocked chakras or subdue overactive ones. To choose the right crystal for the job, you will have to take a detailed look at the crystal stones' properties and attributes, such as their energetic quality and color. You will also have to note whether you resonate with the stone or not. That matters a great deal while choosing crystals.

How Can Crystals Help Us Heal Chakras?

If you've dabbled in alternative medicine before, you must have heard about the mystical powers of healing crystals already. Crystals are fossilized resins or minerals that are said to possess beneficial properties that enhance our health. But the question arises: how do these crystals help us heal chakras?

Healing crystals are placed on your body to promote physical, emotional, and spiritual wellness. When the crystals' energy interacts with the life force of your chakras, they result in positive outcomes for your body. They are believed to alleviate stress and enhance concentration and creativity.

Feeling a personal connection with a crystal is essential. Healing practitioners instruct clients to place individual crystals, such as clear quartz, in their hands' palms. Energy is said to leave and enter your body using your palms as a gateway. Your hands and throat also manifest energy in various ways. These are what make writing such a powerful tool of expression.

There is no perfect spot to keep the healing crystals upon. Your chakras make fields of energy around them, and merely being in the presence of a healing crystal will have a positive effect on their health. Healing crystals depend a whole lot on an individual's intentions, so you can't go wrong as long as you have pure ones!

Balancing the chakras is essential in order to be at peace with oneself genuinely. The inevitable stressors of life often cause our chakras to misalign or go out of balance. Wearing crystals or performing crystal healing practices are said to assist in aligning your chakras in an incredibly powerful way.

What Are Some Useful Crystals?

The seven main chakra wheels within our body are each associated with a certain color. The colors that correspond with the chakras vary from red at the base of your spine to purple at the Crown Chakra. Not only do these colors represent the chakras, they also relate to the functionality of each of the energy wheels.

The Root Chakra Crystals

The Root Chakra is associated with the color red. The stones corresponding to this chakra are also in different shades and hues of red. The crystals that help align this energy vortex are as follows:

1) Garnet
2) The Red Jasper
3) Hematite
4) Fire Agate
5) Black Tourmaline

The Sacral Chakra Crystals

This chakra is associated with the color orange, and its corresponding healing crystals are:

1) Amber

2) Carnelian
3) Citrine
4) Moonstone
5) Coral

The Solar Plexus Chakra Crystals

The color corresponding to the Solar Plexus Chakra is yellow. Yellow stones are widely known for their properties of harmony and prosperity. Some of them are:

1) Malachite
2) Calcite
3) Topaz
4) Agate
5) Tiger's Eye
6) Citrine

The Heart Chakra Crystals

If you want to align this chakra, you should go for pink or green crystals, as those are the colors related to this energy bundle. Some of the stones that you can opt for are:

1) Aventurine
2) Rose Quartz
3) Amazonite
4) Jade

5) Green Calcite
6) Green Tourmaline

The Throat Chakra Crystals

This chakra corresponds with the color blue. To heal the Throat Chakra, you should go for the following stones.

1) Lapis Lazuli
2) Turquoise
3) Aquamarine
4) Celestite
5) Blue Apatite

The Third Eye Chakra Crystals

The Third Eye Chakra corresponds with the color indigo. The stones associated with it are as follows:

1) Sodalite
2) Sapphire
3) Purple Fluorite
4) Black Obsidian
5) Amethyst

The Crown Chakra Crystals

The highest chakra, the Crown Chakra, is associated with the color violet and white. Its corresponding stones are mentioned below.

1) Clear Quartz
2) Selenite
3) Diamond
4) Moonstone
5) Amethyst

Chapter 6: How to Know If Your Chakras are Out of Balance?

The Main Symptoms and Signs of Blocked Chakras and the Problems Caused By It

The seven chakras form a pivotal straight line of power within your body. When this line is straightforward, you will be at the peak of your mental and physical health. Your emotions will be regulated, and you will not feel excess stress or anxiety. You will respond to events in a healthy manner, whether they are good or bad.

But when this line of energy bundles is a little skewed or imbalanced, things start to go wrong. For example, if one or more of our chakras spin too fast, we start feeling hyperactive, tense, or excessively nervous over little things. It can result in us feeling overworked or burnt out. On the other hand, if the chakras are spinning slower than necessary, we experience tiredness, lack of creativity, and mental and physical exhaustion.

The warning signs that your chakras may be off are as follows:

1) You don't feel like yourself lately.
2) You fall sick very often.
3) You subconsciously make mistakes.
4) Nothing seems to work out in your favour.

If you are experiencing any of these, then there is probably something amiss with your chakras. A chakra blockage or imbalance can manifest itself as several kinds of physical and mental issues. These can include:

- *Concentration problems*
  Having one or more of your chakras imbalanced means you may experience a lack of focus and have trouble concentrating. It is because some chakras, like the Third Eye Chakra, are directly responsible for our intellect and vision.
- *A sense of helplessness*
  Blockages in the Heart Chakra can cause feelings of helplessness and isolation to accumulate slowly over time, leading to stress and other mental disorders.
- *Lack of motivation*
  Certain chakras like the Solar Plexus Chakra are linked to one's ability to draw inspiration. When those chakras are imbalanced, they constrict your creative energy. It can result in an individual losing motivation.
- *Trouble sleeping*
  Chakras are power centers that, when balanced, allow you to achieve an incredible level of serenity and calmness. They regulate your sleep and awakening. When your chakras are blocked, you will most likely be too troubled to sleep peacefully in one long stretch.

- *Failure to achieve your goals*
  A blockage in chakras may result in your priorities shifting. You may be overcome with feelings of distress that act as an obstacle between you and your personal growth. It may be a sign of your Throat Chakra failing.
- *Inability to communicate*
  Once again, the Throat Chakra is responsible for how you express your feelings and communicate. If this chakra is blocked, it may result in you being unable to convey your emotions properly.

These are some general symptoms of one or more of your chakras being blocked. Each chakra's blockage has a different effect on your body.

Blocked Root Chakra

The Root Chakra sits at your tailbone, so an imbalance in this chakra results in problems in your legs, feet, tailbone, and your immune system. A blockage of this chakra may manifest physical illnesses like arthritis and eating disorders. Its emotional consequences may include a lack of survival instincts and feeling constantly insecure or nervous.

Blocked Sacral Chakra

A blockage in this chakra may result in sexual issues, along with urinary diseases and kidney dysfunctions. Lower back pain and reproductive problems may arise, as well. An imbalanced Sacral Chakra affects our creativity, pleasure, and ability to express ourselves sexually. You will experience a spike in fear of impotence and betrayal within relationships.

Blocked Solar Plexus Chakra

An imbalance in the Solar Plexus Chakra results in digestive issues, liver problems and high blood pressure, diabetes, and colon diseases. You may also experience chronic fatigue and stomach ulcers if your Solar Plexus Chakra is out of balance. Emotionally, you may experience a sense of powerlessness and low self-esteem. You might notice a spike in fears of rejection and critique, too.

Blocked Heart Chakra

The physical signs of a blocked Heart Chakra include heart problems, asthma, and lymphatic systems dysfunctions. You will also feel upper back and shoulder pains. The emotional results of an imbalance in this chakra results in feelings of bitterness and jealousy and loneliness, and isolation. You may also feel a lack of empathy towards others and yourself.

Blocked Throat Chakra

When your Throat Chakra is blocked, you may notice an increase in sore throats, thyroid issues, and ear infections. You will also experience neck and shoulder pain, along with symptoms of laryngitis and ulcers. Emotionally, you will feel misunderstood and secretive, and will have difficulty speaking your truth.

Blocked Third Eye Chakra

A blocked Third Eye Chakra results in poor judgment and lack of focus. You will suffer from headaches and eyesight problems like blurred vision and eyestrain. You may experience hearing loss and sinus issues, too.

Blocked Crown Chakra

An unbalancing of the Crown Chakra will manifest itself as depression and sensitivity to light and sound. You may experience learning difficulties and an intense fear of alienation. You will also have rigid thoughts regarding faith and spirituality.

Main Symptoms and Signs of Overactive Chakras and the Problems Caused By It

Just like your chakras can go out of balance when too little attention is paid to their needs, they can also go into overdrive. When too much attention is directed towards a specific area of your life, your chakras may become overactive. An overactive chakra means an influx of energy is being focused on it, which may upset the entire chakra system's balance.

If you overwater a plant, it will die. Similarly, a chakra absorbing too much energy will have adverse effects. The main symptoms and signs of overactive chakras are mentioned below:

An Overactive Root Chakra:
- Materialistic and greedy
- Lust for power
- Cynicism
- Resistance to change
- Obsession with security
- Aggressiveness

An Overactive Sacral Chakra:
- Over-emotional and forming deep emotional attachments
- Fixation on sex
- Cynicism
- Tendency to be manipulative
- Self-indulgence

An Overactive Solar Plexus Chakra:
- Power-hungry
- Domineering
- Critical of oneself and others
- Perfectionism

An Overactive Heart Chakra:
- Jealousy

- Co-dependence
- Alternating between selfishness and self-sacrificing
- Giving too much of one-self to others

An Overactive Throat Chakra:
- Loud and intolerant
- Critical of others
- Using harsh words
- Speaking too much
- Bad listener

An Overactive Third Eye Chakra:
- Nightmares and delusions
- Obsessive behaviour
- Fantasizing too much
- Hallucinations

An Overactive Crown Chakra:
- Learning difficulties
- Excessively intellectualizing things
- Spiritual addiction and ignoring bodily needs
- Dogmatic and judgemental
- Ungrounded

A blockage in the chakra system may feel like a huge problem, but you can rest assured, knowing that it is undoubtedly a solvable one. It may take some time and a whole lot of mental preparation to undertake this spiritual journey but once you get started, accomplishing maximum physical health and mental tranquility is just a few steps away.

Chakras being imbalanced or overactive is nothing to worry about. An overload of emotion from emotionally traumatic incidents or physical injuries will surely result in your chakra system misbalancing. It may take some time to realign your chakras. Working on your chakras is a tough battle, but its result is sweet and serene.

Chapter 7: Chakra Balancing

We know that chakras are the energy centers in our bodies responsible for transmitting energy to every part of the body. When this flow of energy is obstructed due to any reason, your chakras get blocked. Similarly, the overflow of energy results in overactive chakras, which is also not good for your physical and mental health.

To maintain a healthy and peaceful lifestyle and keep your body in harmony, your chakras must be balanced and aligned. Now the question is, can we balance our out-of-balance chakras. The answer is, yes, you can. In this method, we will discuss various strategies that you can adopt to balance your chakras and start living a healthy life once again. Whether your chakras are blocked, closed, or overactive, these techniques will work for you. The key is to be patient and consistent. With regular practice and dedication, you will be able to reap the tremendous benefits of these methods.

Meditation

Whether you have practiced meditation or not, you must have heard the word meditation at some point in your life. It is one of the most common yet best techniques to heal your chakras. Meditation is all about bringing mindfulness and awareness in your life. Many people think that meditation requires you to empty your mind from all kinds of thoughts. It is not true. Vacating your mind of ideas is a false dream, and contemplation has nothing to do with it. Meditation encompasses focusing on anchors such as breath, sounds, sensations in the body, and even visual objects. When you strengthen your focus and concentration, you are ultimately better positioned to observe your mind, feelings, and thoughts without being judgemental. When it comes to balancing your chakras through meditation, there are two levels. First, the meditator should concentrate on the cause level. Here, you focus on your present state of mind and feelings. The purpose of cause level is to understand how you feel. Do you feel mentally stressed or physically tired?

Once you become aware of your feeling, the second step is to focus on the effect level. Here, you pay attention to ease your senses and relax your mind and body. Whether you are new to meditation or just having trouble understanding how chakra meditation works, a guided chakra mediation might solve your problem. Fortunately, we are living in the age of technology and the internet. There are several guided mediation apps and videos available that you can use to heal your chakras. Just google "guided chakra meditation app/videos," and you will find a variety of options.

Affirmations

Another amazing and powerful technique to balance your chakras is affirmations. Affirmations are positive statements or phrases that help you strengthen and heal your damaged emotions and feelings. Affirmations aim to create new thought patterns aligned with the positive energy in your body. When we repeat these affirmations, it poses a positive effect on our energy centers, i.e., chakras, and hence they get balanced and healed.

While working with affirmations, we focus on multiple aspects, one at a time. Below are some examples of affirmations for the various Chakras:

The Root Chakra

"I choose to trust the universe to guide me. With every breath, I release stress."

The Sacral Chakra

"I am beautiful in my own skin. I am strong and enjoy a healthy and exciting life."

The Solar Plexus

"I am confident and powerful. I deserve to achieve all of my goals and dreams."

The Heart Chakra

"My heart is filled with joy. I love myself, unconditionally. My heart is free from past pain."

The Throat Chakra

"My thoughts are positive, and I always express myself truthfully and clearly."

The Third Eye Chakra

"life's situation is an opportunity for growth. My inner wisdom is enough to guide me to my highest potential."

The Crown Chakra

"I am open to abundance and greatness the universe offers."

These are just a few examples of affirmations. You can find hundreds of affirmations related to specific chakras on the internet. You can also create your affirmations. The key is to repeat these affirmations multiple times, every day with focus and present mind.

Colours

In the previous chapters, you learned that each chakra is associated with a specific color, and each color holds a different vibration. So, when we incorporate chakra-specific colors in our home décor, diet, clothes, and accessories we use, our physical state, emotions, and moods can be positively influenced. As a result, our chakras get rebalanced.

Sound

Just like colors, the sounds also have particular frequencies. When we listen to specific sounds such as music, our energy centers resonate with them. Let's understand it by an example. When someone praises you using positive words, you feel good and energetic because they transmit positive energy to you. Similarly, when someone taunts you or uses bad phrases about you, you feel enraged because these words' negative energy transfers in your body.

If you want to heal your chakras through sound, music can be the best option. Listening to the soothing and relaxing music will stimulate your energy centers, resulting in balanced chakras. One of the popular techniques includes.

Essential Oils

Who doesn't love a soothing massage that relaxes all your muscles and eases body pain? What if the same massage can balance your chakras as well? Amazing. Massaging techniques, if combined with specific essential oils, can do wonders to heal your chakras. The aroma and energy of these oils resonate with your energy centers and create harmony. Following are some of the recommended essential oils for each chakra:

1. **The Root Chakra** - Patchouli and Frankincense
2. **The Sacral Chakra** – Neroli and Clove
3. **The Solar Plexus Chakra** – Rosemary and Peppermint
4. **The Heart Chakra** - Rosewood, Basil and Rose
5. **The Throat Chakra** – Lemongrass and Blue chamomile
6. **The Third Eye Chakra** – Lavender and Elemi
7. **The Crown Chakra** – Sandalwood and Geranium

Chakra Crystals

One of the best methods to rebalance your chakras is to use chakra crystals. The chakra crystals are the healing stones that are available in a variety of colors. These crystals hold a particular vibration that is used to heal chakras. Each chakra can be balanced through one or more appropriate stones. In the next chapter, we will thoroughly discuss these crystals and the role they play in healing your chakras.

Yoga

Yoga is not only a healing technique but also a lifestyle. If practiced regularly, it can positively transform your life in the long turn. It is often said that those who incorporate yoga in their daily routine are more active and stress-free. Why is that so? Because yoga not only shapes your body, it also balances the flow of energy inside your body. Hence, you enjoy a healthy and happy life. According to Yoga Journal, the following poses are beneficial to balance each chakra:

1. **The Root Chakra** – Tree pose
2. **The Sacral Chakra** – Goddess pose
3. **The Solar Plexus Chakra** – Boat pose
4. **The Heart Chakra** – Camel pose
5. **The Throat Chakra** – Supported shoulder-stand
6. **The Third Eye Chakra** – Easy pose
7. **The Crown Chakra** – Corpse pose

The best time to include any of these methods in your routine is NOW. Be consistent at least for a month, and you will be surprised by the change it will bring to your life. No matter how stressed and worried we are, we all want to enjoy the bounties of life. Fortunately, by balancing your chakras, you can fulfill the dream of having a joyous life. In the next chapter, we will discuss how healing crystals can promote a magical transformation in your life.

Chapter 8: Food for Your Chakras

The maintenance of your chakras is crucial for a happy and healthy life. Their state contributes to your physical and mental well-being. Once your chakras are balanced, you will have achieved optimum health and performance. Your chakras are also responsible for your emotional and spiritual health. If these powerful wheels of energy inside your body are out of balance, you may experience several difficulties and problems.

Our physical forms have energy flowing harmoniously through it. As we go through life, emotional and physical stressors end up misaligning our chakras, and the energy dims. It results in various physical and mental health issues, including pain in certain body parts and unwarranted emotional distress. When things in your life don't go well, the vortexes of power within you take notice. If they are balanced, they tend to make you feel at peace with the things around you, but if they are unbalanced, the chakras themselves can add chaos to your life.

This is why it is absolutely crucial to

1) Get your chakras balanced, and,
2) Once they are, keep them balanced.

Once Balanced, How To Keep Chakras From Getting Blocked Or Overactive Again?

Awakening your chakras can be a challenging task. It may take you hours, months, or years depending on your individual needs and lifestyle. However, once balanced, you can achieve a whole lot with your life. The peace and tranquility you feel once all your seven chakras are balanced is out of this world. It cannot be reciprocated.

Once balanced, you feel completely connected to all forms of energy around and within you. You can transcend dimensions and become one with the universe. You are a part of everything, and everything is a part of you. When you breathe in, you inhale the cosmic energies of this universe, and when you breathe out, you exhale them. True inner peace comes with knowing that this universe and everything in it is a gigantic system that you are an essential part of. Aligning your chakras will help you achieve this understanding.

Once aligned, there are many ways that you can keep your chakras balanced. Some of them are:

- *Meditation*
  Meditation is an important part of bringing peace to oneself and one's surroundings. Yogic practitioners and healers tend to recommend some amazing meditation techniques. You may also find some online.
- *Words of affirmation*

Words of affirmation can be spoken, written, or even thought. These are encouraging words that you repeat within yourself throughout a long period, and in turn, they shower positivity upon you. You start to feel more confident and self-assured.

- *Wearing the right colors*
  Wearing colors that correspond to the seven main chakras can be a huge help in keeping your energy wheels balanced. Colors have frequencies that resonate with the energies that the chakras emit. Wearing these colors and keeping them nearby will allow the chakras to respond to them and stay aligned.

- *Music*
  Sound plays a huge part in keeping your energies in tune. Listening to uplifting music, tuning forks, and Tibetan singing bowls can prove positive for your chakra system's health. Like colors, audio also carries a particular frequency, and when that frequency corresponds to that of the chakras, they stay balanced and healthy. These are known as healing frequencies.

- *Crystals*
  As mentioned in the previous chapters, crystal healing is a simple and effective technique to balance your chakras. Gemstones and crystals possess vibes of creativity and positivity. The stones corresponding to the

chakras will help maintain their health by providing health-enhancing properties and attributes. Chakras pick up on their frequencies almost immediately, and you can feel the change as you wear or hold a crystal.

- *Alternative Healing*
Seeking alternative healing helps keep your energy in check. Energy healing methods include yoga, Reiki, Quantum Healing, and acupuncture. Healers are available worldwide who can help you practice these in steps. Reflexology and energy therapy are also known to keep the balance of your chakras.

- *Scent*
Certain specific scents can also endorse peace within your chakras. Burning white sage or lighting incense is an ancient practice that helps you focus on yourself and clear your chakras. These scents bring peace to you and your surroundings both.

- *Practicing gratitude*
Practicing gratitude is extremely important! You can maintain a gratitude journal or take a few moments to yourself every day to contemplate. Reflecting upon your blessings will help you maintain a serene inner environment. It will keep your chakras balanced. You

can also watch videos on how to practice gratitude well.

Role of Healthy Diet and Nutrition to Keep Your Chakras Aligned

Along with spiritual guidance, our chakras need some physical nourishment too. To keep our energy points balanced, we need to feed them with sustainable portions of specific food types. Just like with our physical well-being, eating healthy can boost the energy of our chakras too.

The seven primary chakras each require different nutrients to remain activated and healthy, but generally, the right balance of meat, fruits, and grains will help keep your chakra system stable.

A blocked chakra system results in a series of physical problems like illness and fatigue. Once awakened, the chakra system keeps your physical health in top-notch shape. One of the easiest ways of keeping your chakras attuned is via the chakra diet.

The chakra diet is a simple healing method that keeps your body's energy in check. Each chakra is associated with a different color, which makes this diet incredibly fun to follow. It is easily one of the most creative and colorful food diets you will ever have followed.

This nutrition trend takes on a different food for each chakra. Foods with hues similar to a specific chakra's color are meant to activate and boost the corresponding chakra. Tasting foods of different colors and shades is a soothing way to boost your energy, both physically and mentally.

Food for the Root Chakra

The Root Chakra is represented by the color red and is connected to the earthly elements. This chakra helps us stay grounded and stable, and to keep it healthy, we need to feed it with the following food items:

- Root vegetables, like carrots, potatoes, and radishes
- Protein-rich foods, such as eggs, meat, beans, and tofu
- Red-coloured spices like paprika and pepper

Food for the Sacral Chakra

This chakra is associated with hues of orange, and helps bring control and balance in one's life. The food corresponding to it is as follows:

- Fruits such as oranges, passion fruits, and mangoes
- Nuts and honey
- Spices such as cinnamon, vanilla, and sesame seeds

Food for the Solar Plexus Chakra

The color yellow resonates with the Solar Plexus Chakra and is said to be connected to our self-esteem and ego. Foods associated with this chakra are:

- Grains like cereal, rice, flax seeds, and sunflower seeds
- Dairy products like milk, yogurt, and cheese
- Ginger, turmeric, cumin, and chamomile

Food for the Heart Chakra

The Heart Chakra connects to the color green, and its corresponding foods are:

- Leafy vegetables, including kale, spinach, and cabbage
- Green tea
- Spices like basil, cilantro, and thyme

Food for the Throat Chakra

The fifth chakra is associated with the color blue. Foods that feed this chakra are:

- Blueberries and blackberries
- Coconut water, fruit juices, and herbal teas

Food for the Third Eye Chakra

The Third Eye Chakra is represented by the color indigo, and the foods needed to keep this bundle of energy in mint condition are:

- Raspberries, purple grapes, purple cabbages, and eggplants
- Poppy seeds
- Grape juice

Food for the Crown Chakra

Although the Crown Chakra is associated with the color white, it is not related to foods as it focuses more on fasting and detoxifying. To keep this chakra balanced, drink plenty of water and keep it fed by burning sage and incense.

Chapter 9: Mindfulness

Life in the twenty-first century amongst a global economic crisis and a pandemic is challenging, to say the least. We are living in a hectic world, and worries and work constantly preoccupy our minds. Living on autopilot has become our default state.

We go to work or attend classes, mindlessly scroll through social media, and tap to like our friends' posts. Our lifestyles have become redundant and boring. We have become numb to the wonders that this life offers. Not only are our chakras affected by this routine lifestyle, but we are also mentally and physically in bad shape. Although certain people have a penchant for traveling and living life to the maximum, most of us are either too reliant on our friends' and families' schedules or don't have the funds to break.

We don't take the time out to appreciate every moment we are living in. It is not just boundless greenery and starry nights that reflect this universe's significance and beauty, but it is also the little things, like droplets of dew in the morning or the sun setting on a pink-red horizon every day at dusk. We have lost our connection to the universe, which makes us more agitated and disconnected to ourselves and our surroundings.

Mindfulness is the practice of being fully mentally aware of your present moment, surroundings, feelings, and state of mind. It is mindful of your actions, your emotions, and the reasons behind them. Mindfulness is also directly connected to acceptance. Accepting your situation without judgment or self-criticism is what allows you to be mindful of yourself and everything around you thoroughly.

Mindfulness is a therapeutic practice that allows you to reduce the stress and anxieties of life without any exterior forces. It is the act of being fully self-aware and accepting of one's nature and surroundings. It might seem like a small task, but often we are so delved in our work and life that we stop to notice and validate our feelings and mental health. Studies show that those who practice mindfulness are happier in life and achieve much more mental peace than those who don't.

To be fully mindful, we must be in touch with our mind and body together while keeping obsessive and disruptive thoughts at bay. Worrying about the future in the present is futile, and once we accept that living in the now is the key to a peaceful state of mind, there is nothing we cannot accomplish.

The Role of Mindfulness to Keep Your Chakras Balanced

Although the concept of mindfulness originated from Buddhism, it is tremendously popular with people worldwide today. It is said to enhance your overall well-being along with your mental and physical health. Mindfulness is known to improve sleep, relieve stress, and even reduce heart diseases and chronic pain. The implementation of mindfulness requires letting go of your past regrets and anxieties about the future and ultimately results in a better quality of life.

Your chakras require a balanced state of mind and perfect physical health. Mindfulness helps you achieve your chakra system's optimum health by keeping the negative energy within and outside you at bay.

The swirling wheels of energy inside our bodies are what connect our bodies to our consciousness. For them to collectively function, we need to spend some time and effort to feed them. When the chakras are aligned, they soothe our inner struggles and physical ailments. Mindfulness is an incredibly useful technique to help our chakras maintain their balance. Increasing the consciousness of our chakras via mindfulness practices will help them remain stable and awakened.

Mindfulness is about experiencing the present moment and doing, which aids in keeping our energy wheels balanced and spinning. Some mindfulness tips on how to balance the seven main chakras are as follows:

1) *The Root Chakra*
   The Root Chakra is where our irrational fears and worries stem from. To overcome these, one mindfulness trick is to ask yourself if all the things you are worrying about will still be of meaning five years from now. Spend your energies trying to be more realistic instead of focusing on adverse outcomes. Understand

that the universe brings you exactly what you need at a specific time, whether you like it or not.

2) *The Sacral Chakra*
To keep your Sacral Chakra balanced, be aware of the guilt that you have internalized and accumulated in the past. Forgive yourself for your mistakes and try to grow from the lessons that you have learned. Allow yourself to enjoy life without mental restrictions.

3) *The Solar Plexus Chakra*
To keep your Solar Plexus Chakra balanced, allow yourself to reconnect with yourself now and then. Internal reflection is essential to keep this chakra upright. Find ways to connect to your life's purpose and allow yourself to come to peace with your place in this world.

4) *The Heart Chakra*
The heart chakra is an important wheel of energy, and thus requires special attention. Be mindful of the losses and the people that you are grieving for. Allow yourself to grieve only as much as is necessary, and then attach yourself to love and friendships again. Learn to control the love that you pour inside other people.

5) *The Throat Chakra*

Speech and expression of self are an essential part of expelling negative energies. To keep the Throat Chakra balanced, we must be mindful of our internalized denials and dishonesty. Speaking what we only think and believe to be true is essential to bringing peace to ourselves.

6) The Third Eye Chakra
This chakra allows us to be wise and intuitive. To keep the Third Eye Chakra activated, one must improve their connection to the world around us by releasing prejudices and regrets into the universe. Be mindful of your visions and gut feelings. Trust your intuition in every circumstance.

7) *The Crown Chakra*
To maintain the stability of your Crown Chakra, you must let go of all your attachments and restrictions. Allow yourself to be who you truly wish to be. Allow the energy particles inside of you to evolve with the state of your body and mind. Tap into the power of meditation and feel the peace of a balanced chakra system flow smoothly throughout your body.

Meditation as A Way to Practice Mindfulness

Mindfulness is about focusing on the present moment and ridding yourself of all thoughts and feelings about the past and the future. A simple and easy way to learn how to be mindful is through the healing practice of meditation.

Meditation means to take some time out of your busy schedule and internally reflect. Close yourself off from distractions, and allow your mind to wander towards freedom and peace. When we meditate, our minds venture into a tranquil state. We are hyper-aware of our sensations, emotions, and thoughts.

Meditation is a wonderful and easy way to embrace mindfulness. To mindfully meditate, one must suspend their internal judgment and self-doubt. Allow yourself to be naturally curious about the energies and processes around you. Get to know the inner workings of your mind approach your surroundings with warmth and kindness.

Mindfulness meditation allows you to be conscious of the parts of your mind that are inactive when you are mindlessly going through your day's motions. A simple step-by-step guide to achieve mindfulness through meditation is detailed below:

1. Sit down in a stable and solid place. You can choose to sit wherever you are most comfortable, as long as you feel grounded and steady.
2. Make sure that your feet are touching the floor. Take note of your legs and if they are situated comfortably.

Change your position if your legs feel even a little bit uncomfortable.
3. Straighten your back. You don't have to sit too stiffly, and you can allow your shoulders to relax.
4. Position your arms parallel to your body, and then allow them to drop. This action will enable them to fall at just the right place on top of your legs.
5. Let your chin fall a little lower, and your gaze point downwards. It is unnecessary to close your eyes while meditating, but you can choose to do so if it allows you to feel calm.
6. Relax. Feel the world around you slow down. Pay attention to your breathing and the other sensations you feel within your body.
7. Follow your breathing pattern. Take note of your inhaling and exhaling.
8. Allow your mind to wander. After a few minutes of this quiet exploration, return your focus to your breathing.
9. Pause before you make physical adjustments, like scratching your nose or relieving an itch.
10. Once you feel ready, lift your gaze gently upwards. Slowly assimilate to your surroundings by listening to the sounds around you. Let your feelings and emotions slowly re-enter your mindscape.

Chapter 10: Yoga Poses to Align Your Chakras

When we live in a polluted and stressful environment or when our lifestyle is unhealthy due to the consumption of alcoholic drinks and processed food, it can lead to several emotional, mental, or even physical imbalances. Or in other words, we can say it can result in disharmony in one or many of our chakras. Eventually, the imbalance becomes apparent in symptoms like anxiety, inactivity, digestive or other health issues. Though we have talked a lot about different methods of balancing our chakras, yoga is one of the best techniques that can revitalize you from inside out. If practiced regularly, you will be amazed by its benefits. A well-rounded chakra yoga practice can be followed to unblock the chakras so that *prana,* i.e., energy inside you, can move freely through the body. This routine can comprise particular postures, breathing, and meditation practices to clean all the chakras or only those that need to be rebalanced.

Seven Yoga Poses to Balance Your Chakras

The following are the seven best yoga postures, one for each chakra to help you balance the flow of energy in your body. Practice them regularly to enjoy their remarkable benefits. If you are a beginner to physical exercises, especially yoga, don't be too hard on yourself. Move your body as much as you can. With practice, you will master these poses.

Mountain Pose for Root Chakra

The Root Chakra is located at the base of the spine. The root chakra absorbs grounding energy from the earth to feel more connected, secure, and facilitated. When our root chakra is blocked or overactive, it leads to imbalances in our physical body and a lack of sense of security. Mountain Pose is a proper posture to reconnect us to the earth energy. It helps us attract that energy upward to feel nourished and stimulated.

How to Practise

- Start by standing with your feet slightly apart
- Press your feet firmly into the yoga mat
- Loosen your shoulders and reach the top of your head toward the sky
- Put your palms together at heart centre
- Breathe deeply and feel your feet connecting down to the earth and the top of your head reaching up to the sky
- Focus on the energetic connection with the earth and the sky simultaneously
- Visualize your root chakra as a bright red light shining out from the end of your tailbone
- Feel free to close your eyes and take a few deep breaths before releasing the pose[1]

Revolved Triangle Pose for Sacral Chakra

The sacral chakra is located in the pelvic area. This chakra is responsible for self-expression, emotions, and pleasure. When this chakra is blocked or overactive, it can make us feel sexually unsatisfied, emotionally suppressed, and unable to find our vision in life. The good news is, this chakra can be

---

[1] Yogi Approved. (2020). Align Your Chakras with These 7 Chakra Yoga Poses. Website. Retrieved from: https://www.yogiapproved.com/yoga/chakra-yoga-chakra-alignment/

rebalanced through revolved triangle yoga pose. This posture activates the abdominal organs to stimulate the circulation of energy within our sacral chakra. It also helps us act sensibly and live in the present moment.

How to Practise

- Start by standing with your feet about 3 feet apart. Turn your left foot inward about 60 degrees, and turn your right foot outward 90 degrees.
- Adjust your hip and slowly twist your torso to the right.

- Slowly extend your right arm to the sky so your right shoulder stacks on top of your left
- Continue to breathe as you inhale to lengthen your spine and exhale to twist
- Visualize an orange glowing light emerging from your reproductive organ
- If you feel comfortable in this pose, slowly shift your gaze toward your right hand
- Hold for a few breaths and release
- Repeat on the opposite side[2]

Boat Pose for Solar Plexus Chakra

Our solar plexus chakra is responsible for linking us to solar energy, which brings a sense of determination, self-control, and an internal warmth within our belly. Located at the navel center, the solar plexus plays a significant role in shaping our identity, personality, and ego. If solar plexus chakra is out of balance, it can result in low self-esteem and stress. Boat Pose is a beneficial yoga pose to clear our energy blocks and imbalances.

---

[2]Yogi Approved. (2020). Align Your Chakras with These 7 Chakra Yoga Poses. Website. Retrieved from: https://www.yogiapproved.com/yoga/chakra-yoga-chakra-alignment/

How to Practise

- Begin by sitting with your knees bent and your feet on the mat
- Place your hands behind your hips, lift your chest, and lengthen your spine
- If you are comfortable and want to add more intensity, extend your arms forward and lift your shins, so they are parallel with the mat
- Visualize a subtle yellow light building your internal fire
- Hold your variation of Boat Pose for 15 to 30 seconds
- Gently release and repeat 3 to 5 times[3]

---
[3] Yogi Approved. (2020). Align Your Chakras with These 7 Chakra Yoga Poses. Website. Retrieved from: https://www.yogiapproved.com/yoga/chakra-yoga-chakra-alignment/

Low Lunge for Heart Chakra

When balanced, the heart chakra allows us to feel kindness, compassion, empathy, respect, and a connection with others. Everyone needs unconditional love in their lives to feel the sense of fulfillment, and the heart chakra is our doorway to allowing love into our lives.

By keeping the heart chakra aligned, we become able to give and receive love and develop our spirituality. So, let's start practicing it today.

How to Practise

- Start by downward facing dog pose
- Step your right foot forward between your hands and lower your left knee to the ground
- Keep your hips square to the front of the mat

- Shift your weight forward into your right foot to allow your hips to release and to stretch the front of your left hip
- Reach your right hand toward the sky and bring your left hand to your left leg. This variation is a heart opener and also stretches the front body
- Inhale to lift your chest and exhale to find a gentle backbend
- Focus on the heart space and visualize a vibrant green light filling your body with love, compassion, and kindness
- Hold for a few breaths, then slowly release
- Repeat on the opposite side[4]

Easy Pose for Throat Chakra

The Throat Chakra helps us interact authentically with ourselves and others. The Throat Chakra can significantly influence our personality traits, such as confidently communicating with others. When imbalanced, the throat chakra can lead us to experience ear, nose, and throat problems and a block of creativity and originality. The easy pose can help us realign our throat chakra.

---

[4]Yogi Approved. (2020). Align Your Chakras with These 7 Chakra Yoga Poses. Website. Retrieved from: https://www.yogiapproved.com/yoga/chakra-yoga-chakra-alignment/

How to Practise

- Begin by sitting on a yoga mat with your legs stretched in front of you
- Cross the right shin in front of the left, so that the knees stack over the feet
- Rest your hands on your knees with index finger touching thumb and remaining fingers extended
- Inhale to lift your chest and lengthen your spine
- Then, exhale and relax your shoulders
- Gently tuck your chin toward your chest to create a Throat Lock to stimulate the throat
- Visualize a blue light near your throat as it removes any doubt you may have regarding yourself
- While practising this pose, you can chant your favourite affirmation.
- Continue the pose for 3 to 5 minutes and then release[5]

---

[5] Yogi Approved. (2020). Align Your Chakras with These 7 Chakra Yoga Poses. Website. Retrieved from: https://www.yogiapproved.com/yoga/chakra-yoga-chakra-alignment/

Dolphin Pose for the Third Eye Chakra

The Third Eye Chakra is located between your eyebrows. This chakra helps you access clear thought and self-reflection and inner guidance to help you on our life path.

When your Third Eye Chakra is blocked or out of balance, you can feel confusion and physical issues such as headaches, drowsiness, dizziness, and nausea. Dolphin pose is beneficial to increase energy circulation to our face and our brain, which, in turn, regulates the third eye chakra.

How to Practise:

- Start with Downward Facing Dog, then lower your forearms to the ground. Be sure to stack your shoulders above your elbows

- Bring your palms to touch with your thumbs pointing up and your pinkie fingers pressing down firmly into the mat
- Visualize indigo energy connecting your Third Eye and thumb knuckles
- Stay in this position for about a minute and then gently release.
- Repeat 3 to 5 times[6]

Balancing Butterfly for Crown Chakra

The Crown Chakra is the highest and differs from the other chakras because it is not a wheel of energy, but rather an opening. This chakra is responsible for building trust, devotion, and inspiration. It also develops consciousness inside us that connects us to the infinite and limitless. When the Crown Chakra is imbalanced, we may go through spiritual disbelief, negativity about life, and lack of connection from our body and earthly matters. A balanced Butterfly pose can play a significant role in balancing our crown chakra by promoting joy, love, compassion, and connection with the divine.

---

[6]Yogi Approved. (2020). Align Your Chakras with These 7 Chakra Yoga Poses. Website. Retrieved from: https://www.yogiapproved.com/yoga/chakra-yoga-chakra-alignment/

How to Practise

- Start by sitting on yoga met, relaxed
- Take a deep breath, bend the knees and bring the heels close to the pelvic region.
- Keep your heels together under your sit bones and open your knees as wide as possible (feel free to bring your hands down to the mat for balance)
- Once you feel stable, slowly bring your hands to the heart centre
- To add more intensity, raise your hands overhead and hold
- As you hold the pose, visualize an energy transmitting from your root chakra, passing through each chakra,

and rising out of the Crown Chakra as the energy showers a golden white light around you[7]
- Hold for 5 to 10 breaths, then slowly release

You can also add other yoga poses to your routine. Start slowly, and don't force your body too much. As I always say, yoga is not just a process; it's a lifestyle, so be patient with it. Don't expect to see the results overnight. Slowly and gradually, it will show its effects on your body, mind, and overall life.

---

[7] Yogi Approved. (2020). Align Your Chakras with These 7 Chakra Yoga Poses. Website. Retrieved from: https://www.yogiapproved.com/yoga/chakra-yoga-chakra-alignment/

Conclusion

"Opening your chakras and allowing cosmic energies to flow through your body will ultimately refresh your spirit and empower your life."

– Barbara Marciniak

I am glad that you are reading this page. It signifies that you have gained knowledge about a fantastic energy system that governs your entire life. I am delighted that I have become the reason for imparting some wisdom to you. If you have read about chakras and their functions for the first time, you may find it difficult to absorb this information. It's pretty okay to doubt something because it is the gateway to the perfection of knowledge about something. I have become able to write this book after years of research, practice, and practice on chakras. Writing a book is a huge responsibility because you pass on the knowledge to hundreds or perhaps thousands of people through a book. Therefore, I took this initiative only when I had gathered an excellent knowledge about this subject.

Reading this book was indeed a great start towards your journey to healing through energy. However, mere reading will not rid you of your anxiety, stress, and other troubles. You will have to apply the methods mentioned in this book religiously to benefit from them. Moreover, it would help if you did research on your own to comprehend the concept of energy healing even better. I want you to heal yourself. I want you to enjoy the bounties of this life. I want you to be surrounded by positivity. This is only the beginning of this journey; there are many steps ahead that you will have to cover yourself. I am just like a coach who will train you and guide you. However, the practical application of all these concepts is in your hands. I wish you all the best for the day when you will be healed and help others in healing.

PART TWO

Introduction

The absolute best thing you could do to keep your energetic system in check is to perform a regular chakra tune-up. As our dynamic 'organs,' the chakras work alongside our physical, emotional, and mental. These chakras both influence and are influenced by our daily activities and even our nutrition.

We cannot shut our chakras off, just like we can't shut off our organs, and just like our physical organs, our chakras too can get fatigued and depleted over time. If we are exposed to too many low frequencies, such as traumatic events, lack of self-care, and reduced stress management, our chakras can also be blocked. It causes all kinds of different symptoms, such as physical pain and feelings of depression, to name a few.

Thankfully, there are numerous different ways through which you can cleanse and revitalize your chakras. One of the easiest ways to do this is through crystals. Crystals affect our chakras by lifting their vibration, clearing them, and spinning at an optimal rate.

Crystals possess higher vibrational frequencies, and just being around them and setting your intention to attune to their vibration can profoundly affect your overall health. Additionally, each crystal has its exclusive energetic properties and can thus be used strategically to enhance lethargy and subdue overactivity in the chakras.

Through this book, I aim to highlight how you can use crystals to heal your chakras. Remember that you can get as fancy when it comes to crystal healing as you like; however, do not confuse fanciness with effectiveness.

A Brief History of the Chakras

Before you begin any journey, it is essential to know where you are starting. Learning to recognize all the different chakras within yourself and all others will help you transform how you spend your life in this world. However, to understand, heal, and balance the chakras, it is imperative to know what you are studying precisely. So let us first start with a brief history of the chakra system.

The Vedas, written from 2000 to 600 B.C., depicts the Aryans invading India on chariots. The original word 'cakra' or 'chakra' is written in the text. The meaning of chakras is a wheel, and it refers to the wheels of the chariots that this group of individuals used. This wheel is crucial as it represents the eternal and cyclical nature of time.

The sun, whose path is also cyclical, is the center of balance for our planet. In this manner, the wheel, or chakras, is symbolic of celestial order and stability in our personal lives. Chakras are again mentioned in the Yoga Upanishads (circa 600 A.D), and in the Yoga Sutras of Patanjali (circa 200 B.C). In the 10th century, a text Gorakshashatakam was written, which explains numerous meditation techniques related to the chakras.

The primary texts explaining the chakras were the Sat-Cakra-Nirupana, written in 1577, along with the Padaka-Pancaka of the 10th century. Both of these texts describe the seven chakra centers and practices related to maintaining and restoring balance. Arthur Avalon also translated these texts into English in 1919 in his book "The Serpent Power." It is through this book that the Western World was introduced to the idea of chakras.

Chakra Basics

At the core of this system are seven chakras, which serve as the body's basic energy centers. The seven chakras correspond to all the seven major nerve ganglia of the body, which branch out from the spinal cord. The fact that all the ancient texts perfectly described the nerve centers well before western medicine added a level of credibility to the system of chakras and related sister sciences.

The six lower chakras, except the crown, have three major energy channels that run through them, known as Nadis. Susumna is one of the most efficient for carrying energy as it runs up and down the spine. The Ida Nadi crisscrosses through the chakras and passes them through the left nostril.

The Pingala Nadi also weaves a pattern through the chakras, which passes through the right nostril. In a healthy and balanced being, energy flows uninhibited through the chakras. Nonetheless, most people have chakras blocked by impurity or another, which forces the flow of energy solely through Ida and Pingala, and completely avoids the "energy highway" Susumna.

Both the external situations and the internal habits, for instance, the tension that usually disturbs the body or leads to negative thoughts about oneself, can lead to a chakra to become imbalanced. When the chakras are not balanced correctly, your body does not work as efficiently as possible, forcing some chakras to overcompensate while others are forced into submission. When this occurs, your body pays the price, physically, emotionally, as well as spiritually.

Furthermore, chakras are affected by numerous problems we deal with in life and how we choose to deal with them internally and externally in our communications with the world. As centers of force, it helps think about the chakras as physical locations where we receive, absorb, and distribute all our life energies.

Each one of the seven chakras correlates to a specific function within the body, which starts from the root at the base of the spine and work their way up through the genitals, navel, throat, center of the forehead, and the crown of the head. Once a chakra is no longer functional, the results appear in various manners, which are apparent to the eye.

The chakras rely heavily on each other to function properly. It is just impossible to find the right balance even if one chakra is overlooked. The ultimate goal is to bring the balance, which is known as Sattva, to all the chakras through a blend of activity and passivity, which leads to harmony and balance in your life. When this balance takes place, not only will your body function correctly, but your mind and spirit will also be freed, which allows you to live in a state of profound gratitude and joy. The beauty of this entire process is that it affects not only your life but also the lives of all those who are around you.

Understanding the Seven Chakras

1st Chakra: Muladhara: "Root Center"

Muladhara chakra, or the root center, is the foundation that supports our physical life. Therefore, it is essential to keep it strong and stable. This chakra helps our physical body and all the different energies and consciousness that need a body to unfold.

This chakra is situated at the root of our vertical axis, the spine, and is associated with the four basic instincts food, sleep, sex, and self-preservation.

1. Location: Base of spine
2. Function: Keeping you grounded and efficient, desire to procreate, and want of material security; creating loyalty

3. Element: Earth
4. Color: Red
5. Mantra: "I Am Here"

2ND Chakra: Svadhishthana: "Abode Of the Self" or "Identity Chakra"

The svadhisthana chakra is connected with water. This energy center offers uninterrupted access to flow, flexibility, plus fun. While working with this chakra, you are going to address your relationship with both others as well as yourself.

1. Location: Basin of the pelvis around the genital area and below the navel
2. Function: Source of our sexuality, desires, lusts, and greed. Drives our creativity, sense of self, and relationships with others.

3. Element: Water
4. Color: Orange
5. Mantra: "I Want"

3rd Chakra: Manipura: "Gem Center"

The third chakra, which is known as Manipura, translates as "lustrous gem." This is the real Sanskrit name for the Solar Plexus chakra. It is situated around the navel in the solar plexus area and up to the breastbone; it is also a source of personal power and governs self-esteem, warrior energy, and the ultimate power of transformation. The Manipura chakra moreover also controls metabolism and digestion.

1. Location: Navel, specifically around the solar plexus, and the digestive system
2. Function: Source of the emotions, feelings, intuitions, harmony, as well as transformation. Determines

whether a person feels introverted or extroverted, self-confident or unconfident.

3. Element: Fire
4. Color: Yellow
5. Mantra: "I Can"

4th Chakra: Anahata: "Un-Struck" or "Un-hurt", Heart Center

The primary purpose of the heart chakra is connection through feeling. Through the heart chakra we truly feel the link to our soul and the greater meaning of life. As individuals, we feel like part of a bigger unity of all life and realize that all is interconnected within a complicated web of relationships.

1. Location: Heart
2. Function: Source of compassion and unconditional love translating into one's ability to share and serve selflessly.

3. Element: Air
4. Color: Green
5. Mantra: "I Give And Receive Love"

5th Chakra: Vishuddha: "Control Center" or "Purification"

The Throat chakra is the fifth chakra. This chakra is situated at the center of the neck at the throat level and is the passageway of the energy between the lower body parts and the head. The purpose of the Throat chakra is entirely driven by the principle of expression as well as communication.

1. Location: Neck, throat, jaw, and mouth
2. Function: Creation of separate voice and communiqué, as well as ability to listen to others, helps one to accept compliments as well as criticism with ease.

3. Element: Sound or Ether (clear sky beyond clouds)
4. Color: Blue
5. Mantra: "I Speak"

6th Chakra: Ajna: "Third Eye" or "Command Center"

The gift of this chakra sees both the inner as well as the outer worlds. The energy of this chakra helps us experience clear thoughts and gifts of spiritual contemplation and self-reflection. Through this gift of seeing, we can successfully internalize the outer world, and through symbolic language, we can externalize the inner world.

1. Location: Between and slightly above the eyes; the center of the brain

2. Function: Self-realization and intuition, seeing the "big picture" as well as beyond the physical (clairvoyance, telepathy, intuition, dreaming, imagination, visualization)
3. Element: Light or Bliss (Mahat)
4. Color: Indigo
5. Mantra: "I See"

7th Chakra: Sahasrara: "Unbound" or "Infinite", the Seat Of The Soul

The seventh chakra is the crown chakra. This chakra is positioned at the top of the head; it gives us access to higher cognizance states as we open to what is beyond our fixations and visions. The function of this chakra is motivated by consciousness and helps us get in touch with the universal.

1. Location: Crown of the head
2. Function: Realization of the infinite, spirit, Divine God, universe, and unity; enlightenment and spiritual connection; ability to receive understanding and knowledge
3. Element: Universal intelligence (Satchitdananda) of Thought/Meditation
4. Color: White (sometimes depicted as Violet)
5. Mantra: Silence

RIGHTS OF 7 CHAKRAS

- TO KNOW
- TO SEE
- TO SPEAK
- TO LOVE
- TO ACT
- TO FEED
- TO BE HERE

Recognizing Imbalances in the Chakras

When a chakra is not properly functioning, it can lead to a ripple effect throughout our lives and those around us. At any given moment, depending upon a huge range of circumstances, both positive as well as negative, the energy in the chakra can get stuck or excessive, which can lead to an imbalance in the system.

Those who are in tune with their system will be able to recognize these changes and begin working towards correcting themselves. These corrections can be done through simple exercises, some life changes, yoga, and meditation, to name a few.

Often, the energy in a chakra is stuck only for a matter of minutes, while at other times, it can be stagnant for years, and sometimes even a lifetime. You can use the following reference guide to recognize the imbalances in the seven chakras. Through this chapter, I aim to show how a weakness, whether in deficiency or excess, in a specific chakra can manifest negatively in your day to day activities.

1st: Muladhara (Root Chakra)

1. Feeling of being overcome by personal life, work, and responsibilities that result in either extreme stress or just completely giving up
2. Stressed due to a "survival crises" health, money, home, and family
3. Piles of mess, "to-do" lists, and chores that don't get moved or accomplished
4. Often termed as a messy and confused person
5. Travel frequently
6. Resilient to exercise, healthy diet, as well as fresh air
7. Gluttony, hoarding money or assets
8. A profound sense of often feeling ungrounded. Living inside the head instead of the body

2ND: **Svadhishthana (Pelvic Chakra)**

1. Prefer solitude due to fear of judgment
2. Feelings of uncertainty or not being safe
3. Feeling "stuck" in your professional or personal relationships, or both
4. A strong desire of wanting somebody to take good care of you
5. Neediness
6. Self-described "overachievers"
7. Growing up in a situation where emotions were repressed or completely denied
8. History of sexual abuse and issues when it comes to expressing alongside experiencing sexuality
9. Chronic pain in the lower back and hips

10. Reproductive health problems
11. A strong yearning to exhibit power over others to create an extremely false sense of confidence
12. A personality subjugated by either shyness or aggressiveness

3rd: Manipura (Navel Chakra)

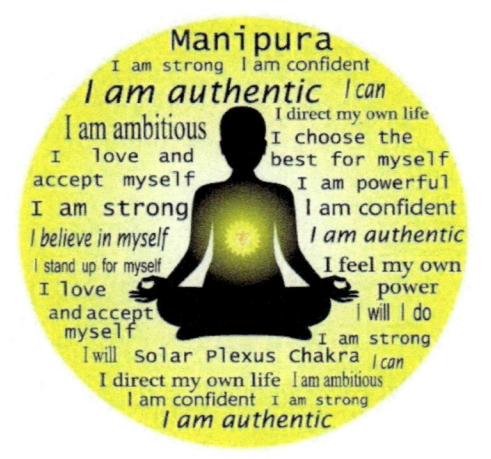

1. A profound feeling that life is puzzling, unsatisfying, and scary
2. Making decisions based upon pure emotion and/or selfishness
3. Habitual bouts of anger, sadness, along with intense emotional pain
4. History of gastric problems and/or eating disorders
5. Extremely low self-esteem

6. Sensitive to a number of stimuli which results in coping mechanisms for instance drugs, alcohol, overeating, and other types of self-abuse
7. A desire to be a perfectionist
8. A compulsive need of self-protection or protection of others

4th: Anahata (Heart Chakra)

1. Regular negative emotional responses to painful or problematic life experiences
2. A life driven by fear or misconception
3. Apprehensions and emotional scars that are dealt with on a consistent basis
4. Failing to forgive or let go

5. Lack of compassion
6. A strong connection to the result of an experience rather than thankfulness for an experience
7. Fear of letting people get too close into your personal world
8. Intense shyness or loneliness
9. Struggle to receive or give love fully
10. Deep misery, selfishness, insignificance, and even hate
11. Shallow breathing patterns, asthma, along with lung diseases
12. High blood pressure and heart disease

5th: Vishuddha (Throat Chakra)

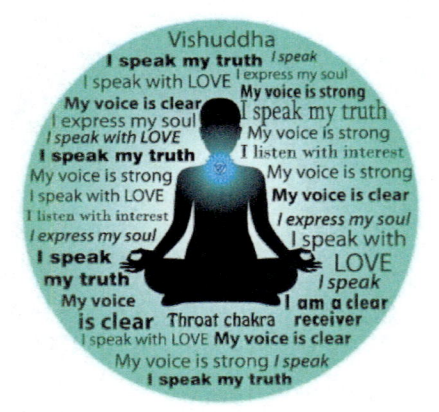

1. A feeling of being insufficient, fearful of making mistakes
2. Abuse of power or lack of power
3. Often surrounded by destructive people

4. A fondness for gossip or habitually speaking without thinking
5. Particularly shy, specifically when it comes to speaking in front of a group of people
6. Struggle with accepting compliments
7. Trouble listening to others
8. Smokers or tobacco users
9. Victims of recurrent allergies
10. Repeated sore throats and/or thyroid problems
11. Stiff necks as well as shoulders, teeth grinding, and jaw disorders

6th: Ajna (Third Eye Chakra)

1. Follow trends as well as people blindly, unaware to possibly dangerous situations
2. Lack of ingenuity

3. Incompetence to focus or concentrate during day to day tasks
4. Find it problematic to make decisions as the situation does not seem clear
5. Oversensitive to the feelings and behavior of the people around them
6. Frequent headaches, hallucinations, and nightmares
7. Poor memory and/or eye problem

7th: Sahasrara (Crown Chakra)

1. An incapability to still the mind
2. A terror to do something today due to a traumatic past experience
3. Acting without the use of innate intuition
4. Apathetic

5. An inability to think for yourself
6. A spiritual skeptic
7. Frequent avaricious urges and shopping addictions
8. Overreaction to ignorance, both yours and others
9. An incompetence to think essentially, almost always resorting on analytical knowledge that is learned from schools as well as institutions
10. Viewing yourself as an elite member of a spiriteable

HEALING MANTRA CODES

ROOT
Muladhara

"I AM SAFE. ALL FRAGMENTS OF ME ARE SAFE. I RECOGNIZE ALL FRAGMENTS OF HIGHER-SELF WITHOUT SACRIFICING MY SAFETY."

HEALING MANTRA CODES

SACRAL
Sradhisthana

"I AM FREE. I AM FREE OF JUDGEMENT. I AM FREE TO MOVE, FEEL AND BE EXACTLY WHO I CHOOSE TO BE. I AM FREE TO CREATE AND ACCEPT ABUNDANCE IN MY LIFE."

HEALING MANTRA CODES

SOLAR PLEXUS
Manipura

"I AM IN CHARGE. I AM THE DIVINE CREATOR OF MY REALITY. I TAKE FULL ACCOUNTABILITY AND RESPONSIBILITY FOR MY CHOICES, BEHAVIOR AND ACTIONS THAT UNHEALED VERSIONS OF ME MADE. I UNDERSTAND ONLY THE VERSIONS OF HEALED ME CAN REPAIR THOSE THROUGH ACTION."

HEALING MANTRA CODES

HEART
Anahata

"I AM WORTHY. I AM WORTHY OF LOVE, FORGIVENESS, PEACE AND UNDERSTANDING. I AM WORTHY OF HEALING. I VOW TO MAKE MYSELF MY PRIORITY IN LOVE, GROWTH AND ACTION. IF IT DOES NOT SERVE THE BEST IN ME. IT IS NOT FOR ME."

HEALING MANTRA CODES

THROAT
Vissudha

"I CREATE CHANGE. THE WORDS THAT FOLLOW 'I AM' FOLLOW ME. MY WORDS CREATE UNSTOPPABLE, POWERFUL AND POSITIVE ACTION."

HEALING MANTRA CODES

THIRD EYE
Ajna

"I SEE BEAUTY IN ALL THINGS. I AM NOT FEARFUL. I DO NOT LET FEAR BLOCK ME OR SWAY TRUTH. I SEE THE LESSONS IN MY EXPERIENCES. I AM NOT A VICTIM. I AM THE MASTER OF MY STORY WRITTEN WITH GROWTH IN MIND."

HEALING MANTRA CODES

CROWN
Sahasrara

"I AM ALL THINGS. AS I MOVE FORWARD, I KNOW, ACCEPT AND UNDERSTAND THAT EVERYTHING IS A REFLECTION OF ME AS WE ARE ALL ONE. I RELEASE ANYTHING THAT NO LONGER SERVES ME OR THE COLLECTIVE IN ASCENSION AND HEALING."

Introducing Crystals and Healing Stones

Crystals, Minerals, Gemstones

Today the common use of the word "crystal" is adopted to cover the many forms of crystals, gemstones, and minerals employed in healing and will be used in this manner in this little guide.

The Origin of Crystals

During history, man has used the power of crystals. Most ancient cultures have held crystals as sacred objects and have used them in ceremony, for meditation, to clarify thoughts, and to heal. Crystals are integrated into our modern technologies, they are used in communications, computers, medical and laser technologies, yet they retain their charm as magical stones. They are naturally shaped by geological procedures and are located worldwide in diverse types of environments. The crystals that we have access to today grew from minerals subjected to strong heat and pressure a million years ago or as a result of sedimentary action over time. Most of the crystals we know about today came from the earth; however, some have arrived here from the heavens or space. These are known as tektites and meteorites.

Types of Crystals

Crystals come in every size, shape, and color. Many are multi-colored. Their mediums follow the modeling of Sacred Geometry. All crystals and gemstones are believed to be living organisms, and they have life energy of their own. They are a valuable part of the Mineral Kingdom, and most are the result of nature, but some are synthetically produced. All different crystals available to us today 'vibrate' on their individual frequency. Numerous crystals are as old as our planet and record their history. Many crystals have a crystalline structure such as clear quartz, while others are in massive form, for instance, the rose quartz. There are numerous crystals found as points, clusters, masses, and stones. They are also tumbled, cut and polished, and formed into shapes such as spheres, eggs, pyramids, wands, obelisks, touchstones etc.

How Do Crystals Work

This might be explained in part through the principle of entrainment and sympathetic resonance: All crystals vibrate on an individual frequency, and we can use this vibration to restore the balance to our bodies as well as our environments, similar to using a tuning fork to match and restore the frequency of a musical note.

Yet another part of the answer is in the creation process. Superheated steam escaping from magma carries minerals that crystallize on the walls of fissures as they cool. All crystals form into an organized pattern, and this structure is why crystals have electrical properties, a fact well known to electronics and computer engineers. The piezoelectric property of a small quartz crystal is what gives your quartz watch its accuracy.

When any crystal is squeezed, it produces an electromagnetic energy field, mostly through the point or a helix. When this pressure is released, it only recharges itself by absorbing free electrons from the atmosphere. This electromagnetic power, or the piezoelectric property, leads to intensifying the aura, or electromagnetic field, giving crystals the ability to help clarify thoughts, channel energy, and heal. Plus, crystals contain minerals with specific healing properties which are reputed to treat or cure specific ailments. You can "tune in" to your crystal and concentrate its power to help achieve your purpose.

A Brief History of Crystals and Healing

It is incredibly accurate to assume that we have had an association with stones and crystals for as long as we have lived. The use of talismans & amulets goes back to the dawn of the human race, but we have no means of confirming how the first of such artifacts were perceived or used. Most early pieces were of organic origin. Beads crafted from mammoth tusks were unearthed from a grave in Sungir, Russia, going back 60,000 years (Upper Palaeolithic period), as well as extant beads made from shell or fossil shark teeth.

Amulets

The earliest amulets are Baltic amber, a few from as early as 30,000 years ago, and amber crystals were found in Britain approximately ten thousand years ago, the end of the last glacial period. The distance they traveled to Britain shows the people of that time their interest. Jet was also common, and jet beads, wrist bands, and necklaces were uncovered in Palaeolithic tombs in Switzerland and Belgium. Xylenol mines have always been in Sinai since 4000 BC. The Christian church in 355 AD forbade Amulettes, but precious stones played a significant role, with Saphir becoming the preferred gem for ecclesiastical rings in the 12Th century. Marbodus, Bishop of Rennes in the eleventh century, believed that agate would make the wearer more appealing, convincing, and for

God's sake. There were also other symbolic examples, such as the pustule of Christ's death.

Historical References

Ancient Sumerians, who used crystals in magic formulae, made the first historical references on glass use. Ancient Egyptians have used in their jewelry lapis lazuli, turquoise, carnelian, emerald, and transparent quartz. They even graved the same gems with extreme amulets. Stones were used mainly for safety and defense by the pharaohs. Chrysolite was used to combat the night terrors and kill evil spirits (later transcribed as topaz and peridot). Crystals were also aesthetically used by Egyptians. Galena (lead ore) had been ground into a paste, using the so-called kohl-eye shadow.

Similarly, malachite was used. The departed heart was generally identified by green stones, which would be included in the burials. To later Ancient Mexico, green stones were used similarly.

A few of the attributes the ancient Greeks ascribed to crystals, and a number of terms we still use are Greek. The name 'crystal' was derived from the Greek word ice because clear quartz was believed to be water frozen, so sublime that it remained solid. Amethyst means "not intoxicated" and was used as an amulet to discourage drunkenness and hake. The red coloration created when it oxidizes; Hematite comes from a blood term. The iron oxide of Hematite is strongly correlated with ancient Greeks rock, the gods of war Aries. Greek soldiers will rub Hematite before the battle and become purportedly invulnerable over their bodies. Greek sailors wear different amulets even to protect them at sea safely.

In ancient China, Jade was truly valued. Some Chinese writings represent jade beads. Chimes made of garnet and sometimes the Chinese emperors were buried in jade armor about 1000 years ago. Garnet masks are found in Mexico around the same time. In China and South America, Jade was known as a renal healing stone. More recently - 250 years ago - the Maoris of New Zealand had pendants reflecting the ancestors' spirits that were passed by the male line for several generations. The green marble practice continued to this very day parts of New Zealand.

Crystals in Religion

Throughout all religions, crystals and gems played an important role. They are described in the entire Bible, in the Koran, and several other texts. The birthplace is Aaron's breastplate, as stated in the book of Exodus, or 'high priest's breastplate. In the Koran, Carbuncle (garnet) is a fourth heaven. The Kalpa Tree, which is an offering for the gods under Hinduism, is said to have been composed primarily of precious stone and a Buddhist text from the seventh century mentions a diamond throne near the Tree of Knowledge. A million Kalpa Buddhas have sat on this throne. Throughout Jainism, the Kalpa Sutra speaks of Harinegamesi, the supreme leader of the foot troops who has seized and cleaned 14 precious stones and only preserved the most refined essence to assist throughout their transitions.

There is also the Ratnapariksha of Buddhabhatta, an essential ancient lapidary treatise. Some accounts suggest it's Hindu, but most probably, it's Buddhist. The date is uncertain but probably dates back to the sixth century. Diamonds are very much portrayed in this treatise as the king of jewels and are classified by caste. For the Hindu Goddess Indra, the Sanskrit word diamond, vajra, is often synonymous with thunder, and thunder is often related to diamonds. The ruby was respected too. He was an unquenchable fire and was intended to protect the wearer's health and wellbeing. The treatise mentions many other stones and their characteristics.

The Renaissance

Throughout Europe, the qualities of precious and semi-precious stones have been revered in many medical practices since the 11Th century during the Renaissance. Stones were usually used in addition to herbal remedies. Hildegard von Binghen and John Mandeville, along with Arnoldus Saxo, were the authors. There are also references to stones with unique strength or defense qualities. In 1232, Hubert de Burgh, presiding justice of Henry III, was suspected of taking a gem from the king's collection, so that the wearing person would be invincible.

Gemstones were often believed to be tainted by Adam's initial sins, to be possessed by angels, or to be treated by a sinner to break from their virtues. Therefore, before you wear, you will be hallowed and sanctified. Today, there is an echo to this idea that crystals are washed and programmed before they are used in crystal cure. While the Renaissance has always embraced the practice of using precious healing stones, the discerning minds of the time wanted to discover how the mechanism worked and to understand it more scientifically.

The Beginning of Crystal Healing

In 1609 Anselmus de Boot, court doctor of Rudolf II of Germany, stated that the existence of good or bad angels was the explanation for every virtue which a gemstone had. The good angels grant gems a special grace, but the poor angels encourage people to believe in the stone alone and not in the gifts given to it by God. He instead calls several stones as beneficial and descends specific attributes to superstitious beliefs. Later that century, in his 'Faithful Lapidary,' Thomas Nichols said gems could not exhibit the effects claimed in the past, as inanimate artifacts. Therefore, the use of significant healing and protective stones started to decline in Europe in the illumination era. A variety of important studies have been done in the earlier half of the 19th century to show the impact of stones on clear-sighted subjects. In one case, the issue believed that the touch of different rocks is not only physical and mental, but also has tastes and smells.

Crystal and Gemstone Meaning

Even though they are no longer used medically, gemstones still have meaning. Mourners widely wore jet until recently, and grenets were used often in times of war. There is a custom in a local family in the southwest of England: each woman's offspring is wearing an antique moon necklace for their marriage, which has been around for centuries. Just a family member recently discovered that this was a sign of fertility.

Until quite recently, if not until now, many tribal communities have continued to use precious stones to heal. New Mexico's Zuni tribe produces fetishes of stone that reflect animal spirits. They were served on polished Turquoise and ground corn consecrated. Wonderful inlaid fantasies are still sold and are rather collectible objects or sculptures, even though they are no longer used much in the spiritual activity. Many native American tribes still hold sacred, particularly turquoise, precious stones. Aborigines and Maoris also have stone and religious activity practices, including some that they share with the world, while other knowledge is still private in their families. It is important to note that, while there is absolutely no overlap between these cultures or the chance of overlap, several examples of gemstones are close to diverse cultures. The ancient civilizations, and even the Aztecs and Mayans, considered Jade a kidney healing stone. Turquoise was worn to offer strength and health worldwide, and jasper almost also provided power and peace.

A New Age Dawns

Throughout the 80s, the use of crystals and gemstones started to reappear as a healing tool with the rise of the New Age movement. Most of the practice came from ancient rituals, with more experimenting and channeling knowledge. The use of crystals was popularized in Katrina Rafael in the '80s, and Melody and Michael Gienger in the '90s.

A substantial percentage of books on the subject are now available, and crystals are also used in magazines and journals. Crystal therapy crosses social and philosophical boundaries. The area of alternative culture is no longer seen as an appropriate, more popular complementary therapy, and many schools now provide it as a subject of qualification.

Different Crystal Shapes

Crystals, especially healing ones, are a great way to boost your energy. Healing crystals have many uses in our day to day life. One of the most well-known and popular benefits for healing crystals is healing the mind and body through meditation. Meditation has long been recognized as a powerful method of healing the mind and soul. Healing crystals are used to focus your attention on areas of the mind that are not connected with physical symptoms or illness.

The healing powers of crystals come from their different shapes and energies. For example, there are healing crystals shaped like hearts, triangles, and spirals. There are also others molded like flowers, angels, and suns. Sometimes, healing crystals are used to connect one's self with spiritual beings or energy. These forces can enhance a person's energy level and bring about an overall sense of calmness and harmony. Crystals can also be used to draw one's energy into the crystal itself, which is called the balancing of yin and yang.

Tumbled Stones

Tumbled stones are a perfect starting point for your crystal journey. The advantages of these pocket-sized crystals are essential for a small sum of money. We also found that several people use a stone rather than the standard energy requirement. Because of its size, rotting stones can be stored in the pocket or purse, placed on the desk inside the car, or under your pillow.

Spheres

Crystal spheres help emit energy in every direction. The perfect symmetry of a field gives the atmosphere harmony, peace, and relaxation energies. Practicing meditation on a globe brings a deep sense of balance, like having the universe in your hand's palm. They integrate your whole being and bind you with your environment's energy.

Pyramids

One of the most efficient tools for the realization and amplification of energy is the pyramid. Several ancient cultures, no one more popular than the ancient Egyptians, have used this sacred tool. They figured pyramids reflect the Sun's rays. Crystals in this spiritual form are meant to use high vibratory energies to increase the strength of manifestation.

Harmonizers

Crystal harmonizers are shaped for mindfulness into cylindrical shapes. Since ancient Romans, these crystal instruments have been designed to cure energy blocks and strength imbalances. Through holding a harmonizer in the left and a harmonizer in the right hand (yin), you revitalize the spiritual energy and maintain a sense of equilibrium.

Cubes

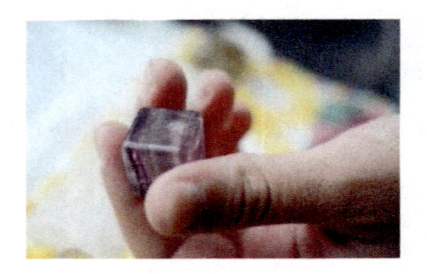

There are several crystals found in the cubic formation. The cube structure is linked to the root chakra. Practicing meditation on cube crystals will help ground your energy and stay connected with the Earth's internal energy. By putting cubic structures in each of the four corners of your house, you will seal, safeguard, and ground your space's energy.

Hearts

Heart-shaped crystals serve to remind you that love is all for you. They are strong allies in helping people to win love and nurture you with inner affection.

Points

Some of the most widely used and useful crystals to work with are crystal points. They are perfect for manifestation, as they help you convey your visions, desires, and aspirations far more easily by transferring your purpose to the world.

Clusters

A crystal cluster tends to occur if several crystal dots grow together on the same matrix. Due to the development of many crystal points, the crystal cluster pulsates at an even higher energy state, directing energy in different directions and working to make it an important crystal.

The Formation of Crystals

What Are Crystals

Crystals are nothing but a group of molecules or atoms. Crystals come in a variety of sizes and shapes, and each one has different characteristics. What they're made from decides how it's going to shape. Few crystals may be formed from salt — these are composed of crystals in a cubed form. Some are extracted from other elements, and they include entirely different shapes. Any examples of such are rubies or gems. Certain factors can produce more than one form. When the carbon dimension is in the shape of a diamond, it could be used to split gemstones, but in many things, we use it every day in specific ways. The most extensive form we use it is supplying our businesses and homes with electricity.

How Are They Formed

A crystal or crystalline solid is a chemical substance whose components are structured in a highly complex microscopic structure, including the atoms, molecules, or ions, developing a crystal lattice that stretches in every direction. Moreover, single macroscopic crystals are typically recognizable by their geometric form, consisting of smooth faces with different character orientations.

A comprehensive research of crystals and their formation is called crystallography. The crystal growth process is called the crystallization or solidification process. The word crystal derives from the ancient Greek term *krustallo*s, implying "stone" as well as "rock crystal," from *kruos,* "icy cold, snow."

Most minerals appear as crystals, naturally. Each crystal has an organized, internal atom pattern, with a distinct manner of locking new atoms into that pattern to repeat it repeatedly. The resulting crystal form-such as a cube (like salt) or a six-sided shape (like a snowflake), -mirrors the atoms' internal structure. As crystals expand, they induce interesting differences in temperature and chemical compositions. But students can never find the beautifully formed mineral crystals they display in a museum in their backyard.

That is because the crystals need ideal growing conditions and room to grow to demonstrate their geometrical shapes and flat surfaces readily. When they grow close to each other, many unique crystals mesh together to create a conglomerated mass. It's is the case with most rocks, such as granite, which consists of many small mineral crystals described above. The museum-quality samples seen in the images here developed in spacious environments that allowed unrestrained formation of the geometric forms.

The internal structure of atoms influences the physicochemical properties of all minerals and colors. Light combines with multiple particles to create different colors. Many minerals in their pure state are colorless; even so, atomic structure impurities induce color. For example, quartz is usually colorless, but appears in various colors from fuchsia to brown to deep amethyst purple, depending on the number and form of contaminants in its composition. Quartz represents ice in its colorless nature. The origin for crystal originally derives from the Greek term krystallos-ice-because the ancient Greeks claimed that pure quartz was solid ice so strong it couldn't melt away.

Scientists usually call crystals "rising," even though they are not alive. They branch and bristle in subterranean gardens, as billions and billions of atoms connect in repeating three dimensions. Each crystal begins to grow larger as more particles are added. Many produce rich in mineral salts from water, but they also grow from pulverized rock and even vapor. Atoms join in an impressive variety of crystal forms, under the influence of different pressures and temperatures. This diversity and beauty of shape and symmetry that the research of minerals has long attracted scientists to it.

Symmetry is a standard sequence of component pieces, repeatedly. Balance is found in nature-a butterfly's paired wings, the whorls and petals in a sunflower, a snowflake pattern, a spider's legs, and minerals are no different. These repetitive patterns exist in crystals within the simple atomic structure and represent crystal faces' design.

You will always see a mineral crystal's signature symmetry from the human eye, but you can need to look at it with a mirror or microscope if the crystal is thin. At first, it can be challenging to identify geometric shapes in crystals, but practice helps: the more examples you look at, the more symmetry and crystals you can notice. Some spec-dimensions, however, do not have excellently-formed crystals and are hard to characterize even for experts.

Crystal Structure

The scientific definition of a "crystal" is based on the microstructure arrangement of the atoms within it, called the structure of crystals. A crystal is a solid in which the atoms form a regular arrangement. Not all the crystals are solids. For example, as liquid water starts to freeze, the transition of process occurs with tiny ice crystals rising until they merge, creating a polycrystalline structure. Growing of the small crystals (called "crystallites" or "grains") in the final block of ice is a true crystal with a regular arrangement of the atoms.

But the entire polycrystal has no recurrent arrangement of atoms, as its periodic sequence at the boundaries of the grain is broken. Most synthetic macroscopic solids are polycrystalline, like almost all the metals, ceramics, sand, stone, etc. Solids, which are neither crystalline nor polycrystalline, such as glass, are known as amorphous solids, also termed glassy, vitreous, or non-crystalline. These do not have a periodic, even microscopic order. There are significant distinctions between crystalline solids and amorphous materials: the process of creating a glass, most importantly, does not unleash the residual heat of fusion, but instead forms a crystal.

A crystal structure (a structure of atoms in a crystal) is defined by its unit cell, a small theoretical box in a particular geographical arrangement that contains one or more particles. To form the crystal, the unit cells are stacked in tri-dimensional space. A crystal's consistency is limited by the fact that the unit cells stack evenly, without any holes. There are 219 potential symmetries of crystals, called crystallographic groupings of space. These are classified into seven crystal systems, including the cubic crystal system.

What Unique Properties Do Crystals Have?

Crystals can have elements called flat surfaces. They may develop geometric forms like triangles, rectangles, and squares. The shapes derive directly from the combination of molecules or atoms that make up the crystal. Smaller and bigger crystals formed from the same molecules should have similar profiles in the very same method. Seven different types of crystal, also named lattices, exist. And are Cubic, Trigonal, Triclinic, Hexagonal, Orthorhombic, Tetragonal, and Monoclinic.

Crystal Collection

Whenever you want to buy something, it is better to have thorough knowledge about it before making a buying decision. The same is true when you plan to buy a crystal for yourself. Prior research helps you open your mind about a particular thing. It makes your buying process easy and adds value to it. To make things easy for you, in this chapter, I am describing the qualities of a few popular crystals.

1. Amethyst

This beautiful purple crystal has a soothing and relaxing vibe about it. It is one of those excellent crystals that you can use during meditation. Its powerful rays help you connect with your inner self. If you're new to spirituality, it's an excellent crystal to get started with.

The amethyst crystal can be specifically beneficial for people with the following zodiac signs:

Pisces, Virgo, Aquarius, and Capricorn.

2. Desert Rose Selenite

Desert rose selenite is a beautiful stone that looks like a rose. Its color ranges from white and cream to brown. It is also commonly known as sand rose, selenite rose, desert rose rock, gypsum desert rose, gypsum rose, and gypsum rosettes.

Desert Rose Selenite consists of calming and rejuvenating energy to relieve stress while boosting your willpower. When you meditate, holding a desert rose in your hand, it brings clarity of the mind and cleanses your body of all negative energies.

The Desert Rose Crystal is especially beneficial for people having the zodiac signs Taurus.

3. Rose Quartz

This crystal is also referred to as the 'love crystal'. This stone is available in a variety of pink colors. Rose quartz is commonly used for attracting and keeping love, as well as protecting relationships. The Rose Quartz can also help to heal your heart from disappointment and pain.

People having the zodiac signs Libra and Taurus can significantly benefit from this crystal.

4. Hematite

Hematite is often recommended to use to ground and balance you in your life. Its color ranges include red to brown and black to grey to silver. If you are under stress and need to feel calm and centered, Hematite can be a perfect choice for you.

This crystal can also help to banish any negative feelings which result from stress or anxiety.

The hematite crystal can be fantastic for people with zodiac signs Aries and Aquarius.

5. Iron Pyrite

The Iron Pyrite is a beautiful crystal with a metallic shine. It's available in pale brass-yellow color. It is widely used to disperse any negative energy or any physical danger. This can also help magnify your intellectual skills and memory.

The Iron Pyrite Crystal is specifically recommended for people with the zodiac signs Leo.

6. Tiger Eye

This crystal is usually amber to brown. It is thought to be beneficial for maintaining and growing wealth. The Tiger Eye is also known to help create understanding and awareness. It can also be a great stone to calm your nerves when you are feeling stressed

The Tiger Eye Crystal can be especially beneficial for Capricorns.

7. Raw Emerald

The eye-catching vivid green crystal is often called the stone for 'successful love'. This crystal can promote focus, clear negativity and encourage loyalty and sensitivity. It creates intense energy in your life that can be very useful to strengthen your relationship.

The Raw Emerald Crystal is amazing for people with the following zodiac signs Taurus, Gemini, and Aries.

8. Citrine

This sparkly yellow to brownish orange crystal is often used because of its warm and optimistic energy. This is one of those

few stones that don't require to be cleansed or recharged. This crystal also helps to fend off any negative energy that comes your way.

The Citrine Crystal can be specifically recommended for people with the following zodiac signs:

Gemini, Aries, Libra, and Leo.

9. Celestine

The Celestine crystal is mostly colorless, but it is also available in red, milky white, yellow, orange, and blue colors. Blue is its most expensive variety. This crystal is excellent for calming and balancing. It is also thought to help people remember their dreams. Celestine can also help provide clarity and peace to your body.

The Celestine Crystal is quite beneficial for Geminis.

10. Clear Quartz

Quartz crystal is a pure and powerful energy source. This crystal is colorless and transparent. It is also known as "the master healer." This crystal is ideal for people trying to get a better perspective and richer understanding. This crystal promotes self-awareness and stimulates your brain. This crystal could be a great stone to use if you are feeling tired, both mentally and physically.

The Clear Quartz Crystal is equally beneficial for all zodiac signs.

How to Select Your Crystal and Care for It

Select the Best Crystal

Now that you know a lot about chakra and how healing crystals can help you balance them, the next step is to select a crystal for you. Whether you want a crystal to balance a specific chakra or get stones for all seven chakras, the choices are unlimited. Several stones are suitable for each chakra. Some stones may have a more significant impact on your than others have. So, the question is how to know which one is best for you? Well, there is no standard rule for it. However, with some research and practice, you can certainly pick the best stone for you. Let's suppose; you want to balance your root chakra. After reading this book, you know that red jasper, garnet, and bloodstone can help you achieve your purpose. So, one ideal way is to buy three to four appropriate stones and see which one works best for you. However, choosing this method will be very costly. So below are some other ways that can be beneficial for you.

Ask the Universe to Help You

A lot of people benefit from this method. They ask the universe to help them choose the right stone for them. Sounds weird? Well, it may seem strange to you at the moment. However, when you enter the world of mindfulness and spirituality, this will make sense to you. When you ask the divine power for the crystal that will work for your highest good, you will answer. Be open and receptive to whatever crystal comes your way first. If you are still doubtful about this method, give it a try, and you will be amazed to see the results.

Use Your Intuition

This method has always worked for me. It is often said that you don't choose the crystal, the crystal chooses you. So, what are you waiting for? Visit your nearby shop to let your right crystal find you. Now the question is how to use your intuition. Now let's suppose you want to buy a crystal to balance your throat chakra. You know that all the crystals with subtle blue color such as aquamarine and turquoise are good for it. But you want to buy any one of them. When you visit the gemstone shop, walk over to the area where there are blue stones. Close your eyes and run your hands over each stone. You can even hold each stone in your hand and squeeze it. Don't be judgmental or get into a pre-convinced notion. Just focus on your manifestation and your physical and emotional sensations. Observe how you feel. Do you feel a soothing heat in your palms? Do you feel some energy charging you? Or do you feel tranquil?

Repeat this step with each crystal and pick the one that gave you the most fantastic feeling. Moreover, also notice that when you look at the crystals, which crystal attracts you the most in terms of shape, color, and energy. Believe it or not, the stone which is right for you will draw you towards itself with magnetic energy.

Choose the Crystal According to Your Birth Month

This is another effective way. Once you are sure about the chakra you want to balance, search for the stone which is best for you according to your birth month and zodiac sign. You can research it on your own, or you can consult a crystal healer to help you with your selection.

Experiment with Different Crystals

This is an excellent method if you want to develop a deep insight about crystals and their healing properties. However, this is a time-consuming method, and you can take advantage of it by observing each crystal's power. Moreover, it is an expensive choice as well. If you are a beginner in the world of crystals and stones, I would recommend you choose from the first three methods.

Care for Your Crystal

It is indeed an excellent decision to buy a crystal to soothe your body, mind, and soul. However, if you want to get the maximum benefits from their energy, you must care for them and cleanse them from time to time. Crystals are potent sources of energy. They often absorb some forces from the environment that may be misaligned with yours. Even when you buy a crystal, it has already traveled long distances from the source to different sellers. Therefore, it is necessary to cleanse and recharge your crystals to restore them to their natural state.

The following are some of the methods that you can adopt to cleanse your crystals.

Water

Water is the easiest and most handy way to cleanse your stones. Water is beneficial to neutralize all the negative energy stored inside your stone. Just keep your stone under the running water or a faucet and wash it religiously for a minute. Could you not rub it too hard? Let the water do its work. Pat dry it when you are done. Avoid using this method for soft or fragile stones.

Salt Water

Salt is a powerful mineral that can absorb unwanted and harmful energy. If possible, collect a bowl of fresh seawater and soak your stones in it. However, if seawater is not available, you can mix plain water and table salt into a container and soak your stones in it. It will remove all the negative energy from your crystals. Let your stones soak for a few hours. This method is also suitable for hard stones. Avoid using it for stones that are soft, porous, or contain trace metals, such as malachite, selenite, halite, calcite, lepidolite, and Angelite.

Natural Light

What could be the most significant source of energy than natural light? The sun's powerful rays and the moon's soft power are the two great ways to cleanse and recharge your stones. Set your stone out before nightfall and bring it in before 11 am the next day. This will let your stone bathe in the light of both the moon and sun. Don't expose your crystals in the sunlight for so long. It will weather the crystal's surface. Avoid using exposing vibrant stones such as amethyst and soft rocks such as celestite, halite, and selenite in the sun.

Sage

Sage is a sacred herb that contains a myriad of healing benefits. Burning sage leaves in the home to eliminate any harmful energies is a popular traditional way. It serves the same purpose for your stone as well. Take a handful of sage, keep it in a bowl, and burn it. Now move the stone through the smoke emitting from the bowl. Allow the smoke to envelop the stone for about 30 seconds. This is the best cleaning method, and it is equally great for all types of stones.

Use Other Stones

Crystals like carnelian and clear quartz are associated with purification. They are considered to be very useful to cleanse other crystals. Stack these stones on top of any crystals that need clearing, or keep them all in the same bag when you travel.

Why Do Chakras Need Healing

Everything in our universe radiates energy, from the most massive mountain or sea, to the smallest blade of grass, to every single cell in the human body. All of our cells emit different amounts of energy, and other cells emit various types of energy depending on when they're in the body and what their function is. Due to the special nature of the body's energy, there are several multiple sockets located at critical points of the body through which this energy can circulate in and out of a continuous flow. They are known as the chakras.

The word chakra means "wheel" in Sanskrit, although it's not like every other wheels we have ever seen. Chakra energy spins outwards as it moves our body's force out and into the field around us, and rotates clockwise to pull the power out of our outer world into our body. It is the intensity state of our chakras that ultimately determines the direction in which our energy will flow, either by drawing power into our body or by releasing it outward. But are our Chakras physical entities? Are the actual little wheels spinning in the seven main centers of our body? No, no. They're not made up of matter; they are energetic. But like a fan's whirling blades, only because you cannot see them, it does not mean they are not there.

You might be beginning to wonder how we can know that there are chakras if we can't physically see them. It's a legitimate point, and one for which science has not yet discovered a concrete answer. It has been studied and demonstrated time and time again during the Ayurvedic and Yogic traditions and in the Chinese concepts of qi and meridians. The influence of our body's energy, the life force that circulates through us, and the quantum field's strength are things that our scholarly abilities have yet to catch up with.

Our chakras exist at seven points along our body, each correlated with a separate set of organs. It should not be too shocking that our chakras' areas directly relate to our body places where the essential systems use a great deal of energy. For example, the one between the eyes sits around our visual center, of course, and our brain's prefrontal cortex. This location is the epicenter of our decision-making, planning, and alignment. There is far too much energy needed in that part of our body that it tends to make total sense to have an energy outlet located in a convenient location. Chakras can either be open or closed, hyperactive, or underactive, depending on how they can flow through them. And that flow is influenced by the open or constrained state of your body as well as energy body.

Chakras and Your Energetic Frequency

The energy from our chakras affects our physical processes through inhibition and relaxation. Note that chakras are like wheels whose function is to keep power going and narrow or close down to protect against negative energy. To account for a small, subactive chakra, another chakra may become overactive, transmitting your low-frequency vibrations more quickly and requires more balance in the chakra healing cycle. That, in effect, generates a lower frequencies reality and extends it. If your chakras are energy centers that emit, absorb, are they the origins of, or are they the product of your frequency?? Are chickens or eggs your chakras?

The double role of the chakras is in the relation between mind and body regarding your consciousness and physical self. When you focus on your body, your mind is on the way, and vice versa. The same goes for your chakra frequency and strength. If you are in the ego phase, it influences the energy flow inside your chakras and the entire physical as well as energy system producing, among other things, more energy needs of the body and chakra.

Only note, if you operate at a lower frequency, then 1) your perception is created, as your five senses pick up what you apply the mind to (This is where we are, all things reinforcing it) and 2) your resonating frequency is what you put in the quantum field and what you pulled into yourself by your chakras, which impacts you.

Balance Is Key in Chakra Healing

No one chakra is stronger or more relevant than others in the energy body balance and chakra healing cycle. You don't want extra energy from the heart chakra and less power from the throat chakra; it does not work that way. Ideally, all seven chakras are cured, equilibrated, opened, and hummed so that energy flows into and out of your body. The remarkable fact is that your body will find a way to transfer energy into it and out (unless you suggest that your ego will stick to it, of course). If one of your chakras is inactive or not, there was an outstanding possibility that another chakra is hyperactive. Since your body needs to maintain energy balance in your chakras, going in either direction (underactive or overactive) in one chakra can have adverse effects and detrimental effects on the energy body and the chakra healing process. The underactive chakra sends another chakra into an overdrive that draws extra energy away from the body. The following examples illustrate how you can behave or feel when your chakras are robbed of harmony and need healing. The first list lists the structural elements connected to each chakra and the possible physical signs that might tell you anything is out of the question.

ROOT CHAKRA TRAUMA

Can leave you feeling unsafe. Nervous. Disconnected from Earth and, therefore, your body. "Up in the clouds." Distracted. But it can also make you feel like nothing ever "takes off." Your great ideas never land or become a reality; you plan but never implement.

SACRAL CHAKRA TRAUMA

Can have you feeling shameful of your body. Disconnected to your sexuality. Dry. Not interested in sex. Lacking creativity. Feeling unnurturing and unable to perform. It can also block affection, abundance, positive energy.

SOLAR PLEXUS TRAUMA

Can have you over indulging in food, drinks, drugs, people, toxic relationships. But it can also have you hiding your true self. Feeling like no one will ever truly understand you or see the real you. You may feel like you need to 'perform' to please others and be accepted. You may base your worth on what you can sacrifice for others and be a people pleaser. Someone who would do anything for acknowledgment or praise.

HEART CHAKRA TRAUMA

Can have you rejecting love and relationships, but it will also have you hating yourself and sabotaging any chance you have at happiness. One may feel heavy; it may be hard to breathe. One may also carry heavy grief and weight from grudges.

THROAT CHAKRA TRAUMA

May make it hard for you to communicate and express yourself. But it may also have you replaying toxic words, self-destructive memories, abusive attacks from others OVER AND OVER again.

THIRD EYE TRAUMA

Can make it hard to see others' perspectives and truths. People can become rigid in their thinking. It can also take dreams, cause headaches, memory block, limitation to psychic gifts, and make it harder to learn.

CROWN CHAKRA TRAUMA

Can make it hard to have faith. Hard to believe in the goodness of humanity and feel one with others in a deeper soul level connection. It can also drain you spiritually and create confusion.

How Can You Balance Chakras with Crystals?

Many times, we feel upset and distressed for no apparent reason. Even after having all the luxuries and comforts of life, we can't feel happiness. We think something is wrong, but we don't seem to figure out what. We often brush such feelings aside, assuming that we are overthinking. However, it may not just be overthinking. You may be going through such emotions because your chakras are imbalanced. By balancing your chakras, you will feel a dramatic change in your feelings and emotions. Balanced and aligned chakras are essential for your health and life. Even people who don't believe in spiritual practices and treatments can benefit from having their chakras balanced. There are several methods to balance your chakras; one of the most effective is balancing chakras using crystals. It is mainly because of the colors and energy order chakras.

Similarly, the energy emerging from a crystal is often guided by its color. Therefore, using crystals to align chakras is very helpful. As discussed in previous chapters, each chakra is linked with different parts, organs, and muscles. A blockage or imbalance in chakras can cause physical and emotional discomfort in its associated regions. There are four ways crystals can be used to put chakras in order.

1. Place chakra crystals on your body according to their respective chakras.
2. Keep chakra crystals near you while resting.
3. Meditate with chakra crystals.
4. Wear crystals.

Before diving into the details of these methods, let's first understand which crystal is best suited to each chakra.

Red Root Chakra

For red root chakra, red or black stones such as red jasper, bloodstone or garnet are suitable.

Orange Pelvic Charka

Carnelian or citrine is the best crystal to balance the pelvic chakra.

Yellow Solar Plexus Chakra

To balance this chakra, the recommended crystals are golden topaz, tiger's eye and amber

Green Heart Chakra

Rose quartz, green jasper, emerald and green aventurine can help you balance the heart chakra.

Blue Throat Chakra

Light blue stones like turquoise and aquamarine can be beneficial to balance this chakra.

Indigo Third Eye Chakra

This chakra can be balanced using lapislazuli, sodalite and amethyst.

Violet Crown Chakra

Clear quartz, selenite, amethyst and diamond can be used to stimulate this chakra.

Now that we know about the crystals that can be helpful to balance the seven chakras let's discuss how you can benefit from these crystals.

Place Chakra Crystals on Your Body According to Their Respective Chakras

This is one of the best ways to balance your chakras. In this method, you place chakra crystals directly on your body in line with the chakras. When the healing energy emitting from the stones enters your body, your chakras get stimulated and balanced. To do this, choose a quiet and peaceful place where there is no distraction. Then lie down on a comfortable flat surface. Keep chakra crystals with you and start with the root chakra.

1. Place red crystal of root chakra at the base of your spine.

2. Place orange stone of pelvic chakra a couple of inches below the navel.

3. Place yellow stone of solar plexus chakra exactly on the navel.

4. Place a green stone of heart chakra in the center of your chest.

5. Place blue stone of throat chakra on your throat.

6. Place indigo stone of third eye chakra between your eyebrows.

7. Place violet crystal of crown chakra above your head. If the crystal is pointed, place it with the point directing up.

Now close your eyes and let your body absorb the healing energy. Keep your body and nerves relaxed. Imagine that the colorful rays of stones are entering your body and reaching every cell. The healing power is erasing all the negativity from your body. If you want, you can also play soothing piano music in the background. (do it before you lie down and keep the volume slow so that you don't get distracted). Enjoy the tranquillity and focus as long as you want. Each crystal has a particular frequency and energy. When this frequency is aligned with your body, it creates a connection between your mind and body. This connection strengthens your focus and balances your chakras.

Keep Chakra Crystals Near You While Resting

Keep all seven chakra stones under your pillow at night or whenever you are sleeping. Moreover, you can keep them near you while resting or reading a book. The energy of these stones is potent. It will keep impacting your mind and body. The healing power of these stones works like a magnet. As it reaches your body, it attracts the chakras, and hence they get balanced.

Meditate with Chakra Crystals

Meditation is an excellent way of improving your focus and mindfulness. When it is combined with chakra stones, its benefit is enhanced. Just hold chakra stones in your hands while meditating. Envision that the colorful energy of these stones is healing your body and mind. If you are experiencing a particular problem due to your chakras' blockage, or if you have a specific aim related to that problem in your mind, imagine that it is being resolved as you absorb the power of these stones. Remember that results cannot be achieved overnight. You have to be persistent and regular in your practice. With consistency, you will experience the amazing benefits of this method.

Wear Crystals

This is one of the easiest ways. Due to our busy schedule, we often don't get time to meditate or place chakra stones on our bodies. However, we can still benefit from the power of these stones. Keep these stones close to your body, such as keeping them in your pocket or wearing them as jewelry. The longer you keep them with you, the more their frequencies will do their work to heal your chakras.

Balancing your chakras will help you become focused and mindful. It can help you understand your inner self. When you are more self-aware, you can find ways to bring peace and happiness in your life. Using chakra stones to balance your chakras can help heal them and bring stability, positivity, calmness, and health to your life.

Chakra Crystal Healing Tips

Functions of Crown Chakra

Crown chakra is the seventh chakra located at the top of your head. This is why it is named crown. This chakra significantly impacts your central nervous system, muscular system, and skin. It serves as the entry point for all sources of energy. It then distributes that energy throughout your body and all other chakras. On an emotional level, crown chakra plays a huge role in connecting you to the universe and the divine source of creation. It gives you an awareness of your highest spiritual self. It makes you realize that everything in this world is interconnected and everything is governed by divine power. When your crown chakra is aligned correctly, you enjoy the sense of gratitude, trust and faith.

Imbalance in Crown Chakra

When your crown chakra is blocked, you feel anxious, distressed, and fearful because your connection with your highest spiritual self is lost. The outlook of your thoughts becomes limited because you are unable to sense divine plans.

Healing Crystals

Two of the best healing stones for balancing crown chakra are clear quartz and amethyst. Clear quartz is also known as the "Master Healer." Its powerful energy helps you achieve spiritual and mental clarity. Amethyst is another strong crystal. Its purple, vibrant energy helps you balance emotions, alleviates stress, and calms extreme feelings like anger, negativity, and anxiety.

Functions of Third Eye Chakra

The third eye chakra is the sixth chakra, located between the eyebrows. This chakra is associated with intuition, wisdom, and sixth sense. It´s the inner eye that gives us insight into our inner self and capabilities. The third eye chakra correlates to our mental abilities, psychological skills, and how we evaluate beliefs and attitudes. This powerful chakra helps us acknowledge the truth and control our minds. When this chakra is aligned, we are focused and can enjoy the benefits of mindfulness.

Imbalance in Third Eye Chakra

A dis-harmony in this chakra impacts your psychological mind state. You experience frequent mood swings and anxiety. In physical terms, people with an imbalance in third eyes chakra often have headaches, blurred vision, and sinus problems.

Healing Crystals

The best healing crystals for this chakra are amethyst and lapis lazuli. Amethyst is also known as the stone of "Total Awareness." It will bring you a perspective that is omnipotent and multidimensional.' Sodalite is a powerful stone to heal your third eye chakra. It comes in different colors, but it is well known for its blue variety. The cool blue rays of sodalite are beneficial to enhance focus and memory. Wearing this crystal also alleviates distracting thoughts and stimulates intelligence. The calming energy of sodalite soothes fears and connects you to your higher self.

Functions of Throat Chakra

The throat chakra is the fifth chakra, and it is located at the centre of the neck at throat level. This chakra serves as the passage of energy between the head and lower parts of the body. The throat chakra relates to communication and your ability to express your feelings and thoughts.

Imbalance in Throat Chakra

An imbalance in this chakra often leads to trouble in communication ability. Some people develop excessive fear of speaking in front of others; while others talk too much or inappropriately. A blockage in this chakra often leads a person to become introvert. They lose connection with their purpose in life.

Healing Crystal

The two best stones to balance throat chakra are turquoise and aquamarine. The ocean blue color of turquoise eliminates negativity and restores confidence to speak and express your thoughts effectively. Another recommended stone to balance throat chakra, aquamarine, is used to cleanse and stimulate your mind and soul. It enhances courage and promotes tolerance and compassion while dissipating fear.

Functions of Heart Chakra

The heart chakra is the fourth chakra located in the center of your chest. This chakra is associated with maintaining relationships, love for oneself and others. It stimulates compassion, empathy, forgiveness, and acceptance. When this chakra is open, you feel content and grateful for all the beauty around you.

Imbalance in Heart Chakra

A dis-harmony in this chakra often results in difficulty in dealing with others. People become closed down and feel jealous of other people's blessings and abilities. They find it hard to forgive others and hold grudges that eventually cost them their peace. Some people also develop codependency. They go out of their way to please people around them and seek their approval. This leads to insecurities and self-sabotaging thoughts.

Healing Crystal

The best healing stones for this chakra are green aventurine and emerald. Emerald is considered as the purest form of green-ray energy. It is also called the stone of "successful love." It can help you bring balance to relationships, encourage loyalty, and enhance unconditional love. Another best stone to align your heart chakra is green aventurine. Its soft energy is excellent for promoting harmony. It is amazing to balance friction or negativity in a relationship while releasing unhealthy patterns and bringing new opportunities.

Functions of Solar Plexus Chakra

Solar plexus chakra is the third chakra located at the upper part of your navel. This chakra is associated with willpower, self-control, and mental abilities. When this chakra is aligned, you feel confident and optimistic about your responsibilities. The energy of this chakra allows you to transform lethargy into action and movement. It will enable you to meet challenges and move forward in your life.

Imbalance in Solar Plexus Chakra

When your solar plexus chakra is blocked, the feelings of helplessness and irresponsibility take a toll on you. You may feel self-pity and often blame others for your problems. In some cases, people become controlling and authoritative over people related to them. Their thoughts are not aligned. They lack clear direction and purpose.

Healing Crystal

The two most recommended stones to balance solar plexus chakra are golden topaz and amber. Golden topaz is a protective stone against all kinds of negativity. It eases fear, anger, and depression. Golden topaz prevents sleepwalking and nightmare while bringing joy, health, motivation, and a sense of forgiveness. Amber is another powerful stone to heal your solar plexus chakra. It promotes healing and renews the nervous system. It absorbs pain and negative energy, helping to alleviate stress. Amber soothes depression, enhances intellectual capabilities, and promotes self-confidence and creative self-expression.

Functions of Sacral Chakra

The sacral chakra is the second chakra located about two to three inches below the navel. The sacral chakra is associated with the expressions of emotions and sexual pleasure. When your sacral chakra is open, you feel motivated and enjoy the bounties of life. This chakra plays a significant role in developing flexibility in our life.

Imbalance in Sacral Chakra

When this chakra is blocked, your emotions get out of your control. Their feelings rule some people, while others feel out of touch with themselves. Some people develop sexual obsessions, while others experience a lack of sexual desire or satisfaction. In short, a dis-harmony in sacral chakra adversely affects your mood and mental state, and you feel agitated and miserable no matter what the situation is.

Healing Crystal

The best crystal to heal sacral chakra is orange carnelian. It has the sunset color, which is very useful to soothe your mind and body. This powerful stone can calm your emotions and boost your intuition, passion, and self-belief. It will also balance the flowing energy while encouraging confidence.

Functions of Root Chakra

The root chakra is the first chakra located at the base of the spine. This chakra is associated with the feeling of safety, security, and survival. It is about your basic survival needs such as food, shelter, safety, and your emotional needs, such as feeling safe and grounded. When your root chakra is open, you feel healthy and emotionally stable.

Imbalance in Root Chakra

When your root chakra is out of balance, you get caught up in your emotions. It leads to excessive negativity and insecurities. Many times, people with imbalanced root chakra develop greed and avarice. Some people may experience eating disorders. Blocked root chakra often makes you feel threatened, anxious, and panicked. Physical issues potentially caused by a blocked Root Chakra include a sore lower back, low energy levels, and cold extremities.

Healing Crystals

Two of the best stones to balance your root chakra are bloodstone and red jasper. Bloodstone is a powerful cleanser and healer that strongly connects with the Root Chakra. It comes in a combination of green and red colors. The powerful energy emitting from these colors represents a blend of growth, fearlessness, and strength. Using this crystal blocks negativity and protects against threats. Similarly, with its spiritually grounding energy, red jasper ensures you remain 'connected' with your real power. It will help your meditation and other spiritual practices.

HEALING MANTRA CODES

CROWN
Sahasrara
I AM ALL

THIRD EYE
Ajna
I SEE BEAUTY IN ALL

THROAT
Vissudha
I CREATE MY REALITY

HEART
Anahata
I AM WORTHY

SOLAR PLEXUS
Manipura
I AM IN CHARGE

SACRAL
Svadhisthana
I AM FREE

ROOT
Muladhara
I AM SAFE

Conclusion

"You have the power to heal your life, and you need to know that. We think so often that we are helpless, but we're not. We always have the power of our minds...Claim and consciously use your power."

— Louise L. Hay

Congratulations!

You have reached the first milestone in your journey to chakra healing, i.e., gaining knowledge about how chakras work and can be unblocked and healed. Reading about chakras is an excellent first step. It shows you are determined to bring a positive change in your life. However, any information is only useful when it is practically applied in our lives. So, the next step for you is to start implementing the techniques presented in this book to heal your chakras. Shifting your focus and awareness on healing your energy centers can boost your overall well-being. But remember that chakra healing is a form of alternative medicine, and every alternative medicine requires time and dedication to show its effects. Therefore, be patient and persistent, and you will experience the fantastic benefits of chakra healing on your physical and mental health.

One of the most special blessings in this world is good health – physical, mental, and emotional, and the purpose of writing this book was to promote a healthier and more active lifestyle.

Being busy fulfilling our lives' duties and responsibilities, our bodies and minds get cluttered with harmful toxins and damaging thoughts. We don't realize, but with each passing day, these all elements affect our lives adversely. Slowly and gradually, anxiety, stress, worries, and depressing thoughts take a toll on our lives. Besides, we also develop several physical health issues. To put it simple, our lives become messed up, and we can't seem to figure out what is wrong with us. Luckily, you are one of those fortunate people who are mindful of the significance of physical, mental, and emotional health. Therefore, you chose to read this book. Developing mindfulness is the key to transform our lives.

Investing some time dedicatedly to chakra balance through crystal healing, meditation, yoga, praying, and affirmations can do wonders to your life. Moreover, by becoming aware of these invisible chakras—and signs of an imbalance—you can try out new self-help methods other than the ones described in this book to tackle your emotional and physical problems. When your chakras are balanced, you will find that your life opens up to new horizons very easily and quickly. It's time to explore your chakras and balance them to enjoy a better and healthier life.

Reviews are an author's sap, whatever genre he writes. They allow him to continue writing more helpful books. Without stars and reviews, you would never have found this book.

Please take just twenty seconds of your time to support an independent author by leaving a review on the platform where you purchased this book.
Thank You!

Sincerely,

Jay K. Morley

Printed in Great Britain
by Amazon